Table of Content:

- Introduction

- About the MIT

- System Requirement

- Application Browser

- Procedure to Make a FrontEnd Design

- Procedure to make a BackEnd Blocks building Without Coding

- Created Model

Have you make Fitget spinner Before or you have been like Fitget spinner, today we gonna be create a Fitget spinner for Android with easy techniques………………

Here we are going to make a Fitget spinner without coding, with logic. This is the way moreover so many people have trying to make a Fitget spinner for android with ease and successful. Here you are the successful person, if you are reading this book. Let go in,……..

Note: Internet Connection is must

System Requirements

For making Fitget spinner for android, you have one pc or Desktop system with the specification:

System Requirements to use App Inventor, your computer must meet the following system requirements: Computer and operating system

- Macintosh (with Intel processor):   Mac OS X 10.5, 10.6+
- Windows: Windows XP, Windows Vista, Windows 7+
- GNU/Linux: Ubuntu 8+, Debian 5+

(**Note:** GNU/Linux live development is only supported for Wi-Fi connections between computer and Android device.)

Applicable Browser

- Mozilla Firefox 3.6 or higher (Note: If you are using Firefox with the No Script extension, you'll need to turn the extension off. See the note on the troubleshooting page.)
- Apple Safari 5.0 or higher
- Google Chrome 4.0 or higher
- App Inventor does not support Microsoft Internet Explorer.
- Windows users should use Chrome or Firefox
  Phone or Tablet (or use the on-screen emulator)
- Android Operating System 2.3 ("Gingerbread") or higher

Step 1:

Open Browser (mentioned in Applicable browser requirements) and Type **MIT App Inventor 2** or search as http://www.ai2.appinventor.mit.edu/

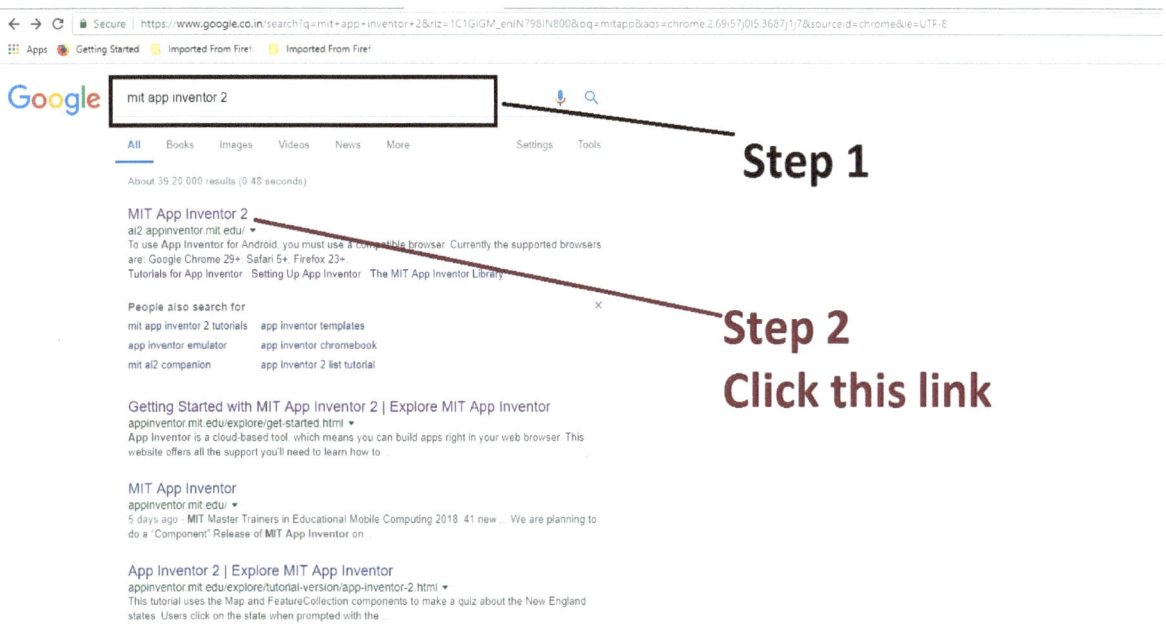

After open this link -→ You can see this login page, below mentioned

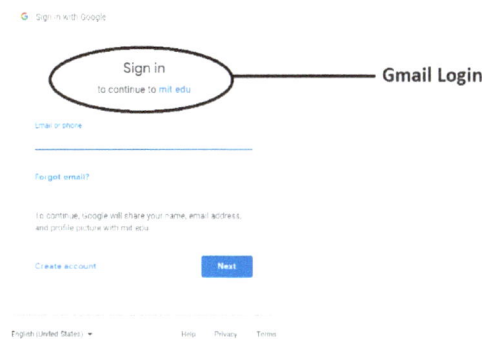

You will see the welcome page, well this page contains three options

Take survey Now --- Which can indicate what are the files and tools are available in that Mit App inventor 2 ….

Take Survey Later --- This option will ask you again and again when you open the mit App inventor 2 whenever using…

Never Take survey ---This will cancel the Survey tour of the App creator

This is not a so much important but it will gain you some knowledge about this online application.

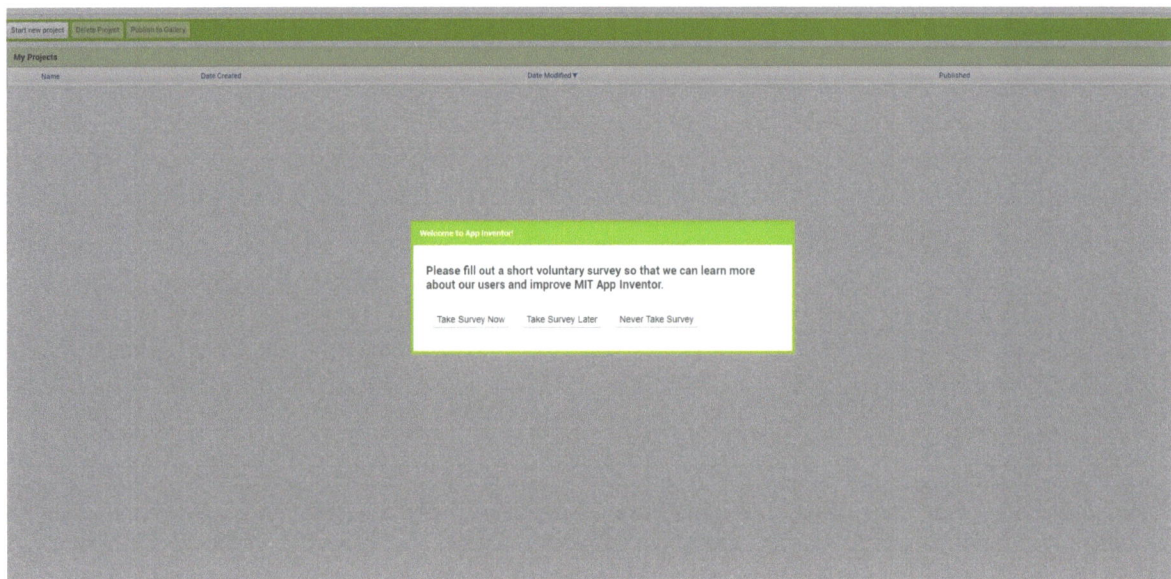

Select Survey Later …………

This window indicates the New updates of This app inventor and also you can connect Smart phone live to this application and check the application live, what are the updates which are done in the application by user. That will see after sometime, we will move --→ Continue

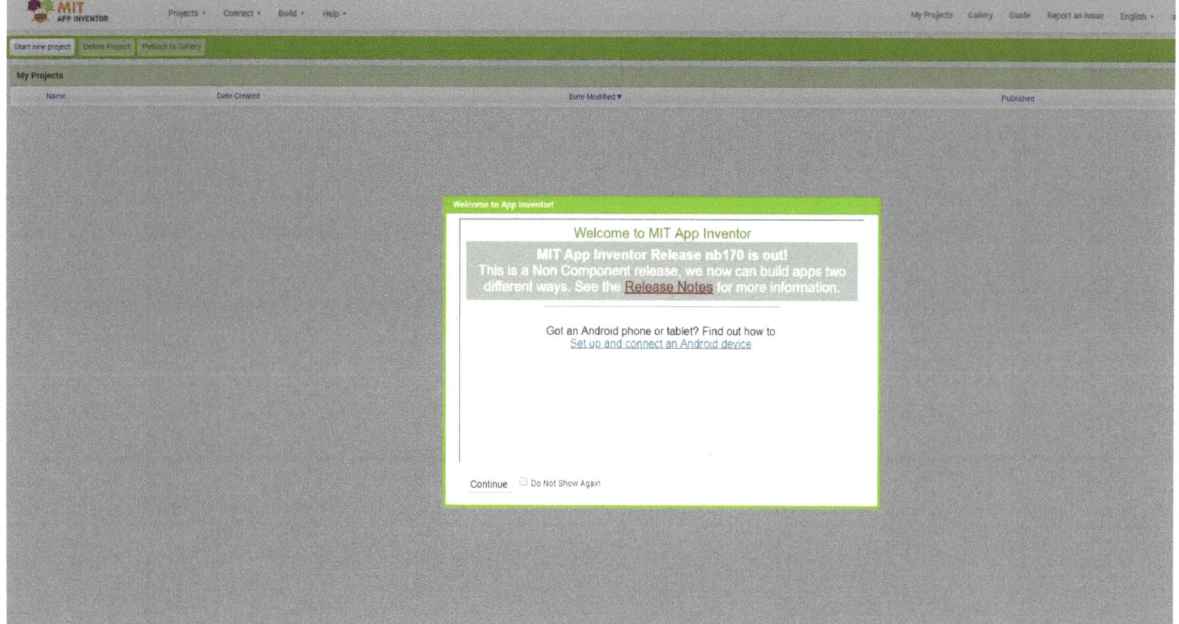

Welcome Screen in MIT APP INVENTOR 2

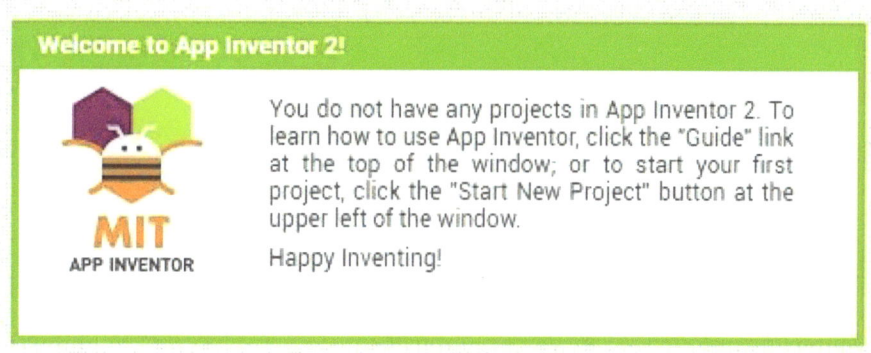

Select new Project:

Project name as Fitget_Spinner, for your convenience user can change any sort of name but space cannot be accepted in this app creator

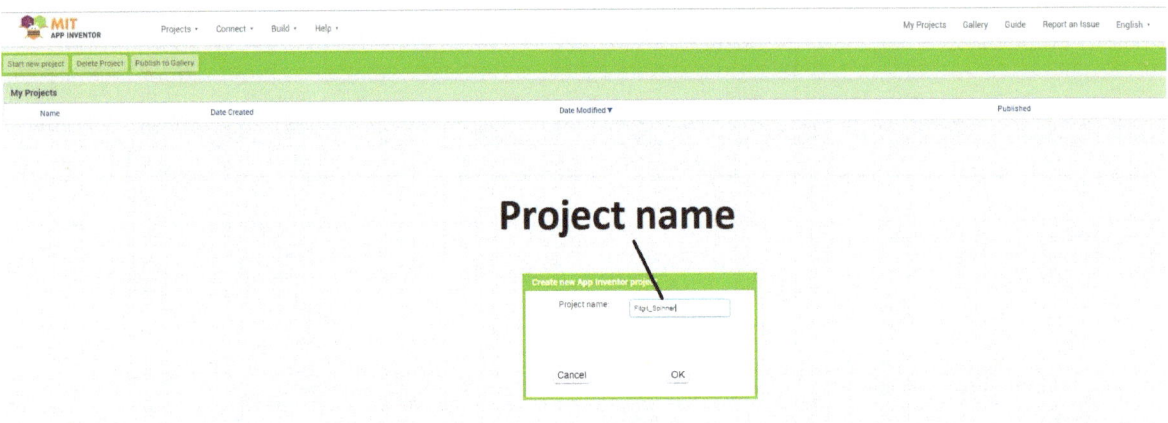

You can see the project page of the App creator. This is the design page, you have to create the front end of the page here

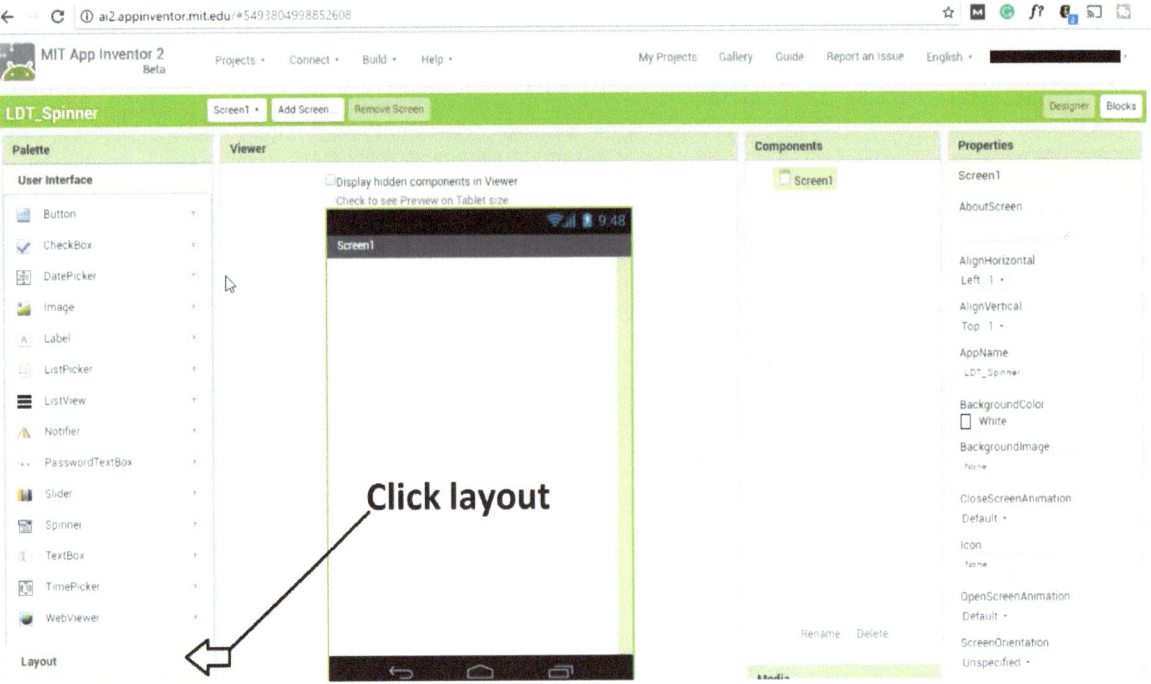

Well, you have to click the (**Layout**) and select the Horizontal Arrangement-
→and Drag it to the screen one by one

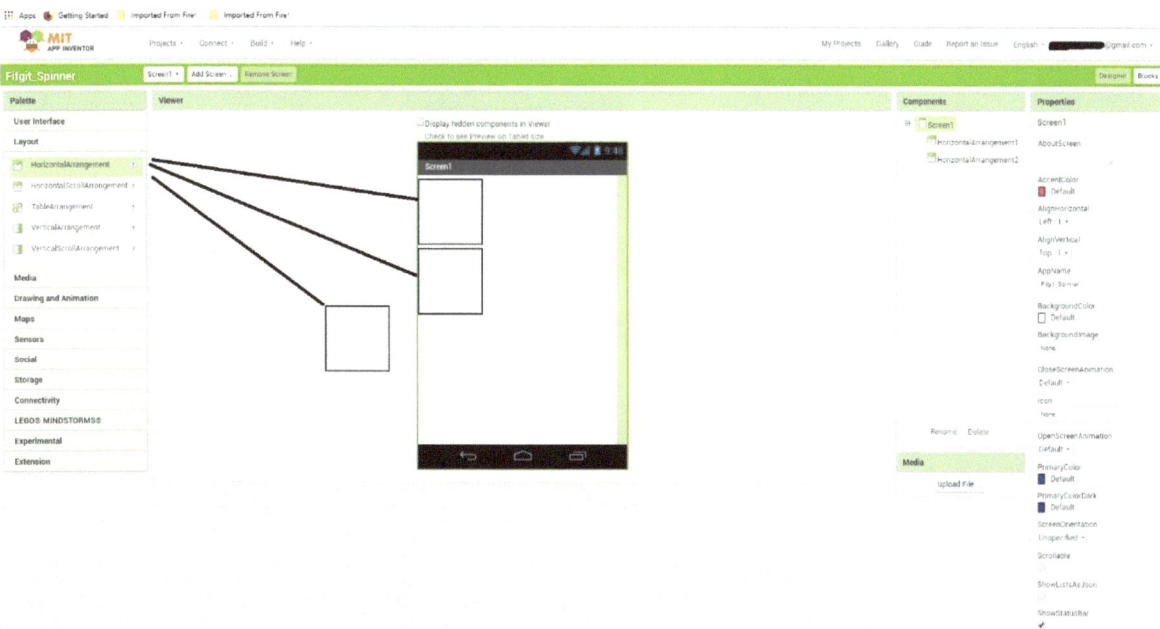

You can see the Component -→ Select the Screen1

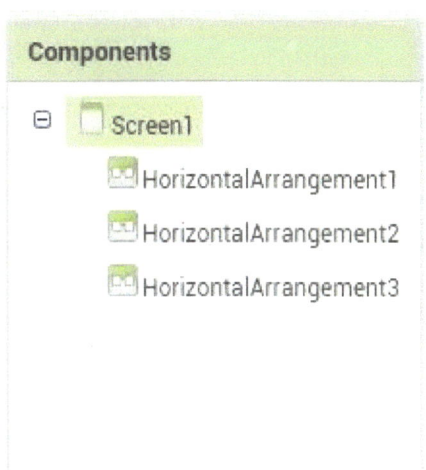

Select screen1→ See the properties → Align Horizontal → Center :3 and also make Align Vertical → Center :2

Now You can see in the viewer panel that the square boxes aligned center

Next Step we have to fix the background color for the screen1. So select the screen1 in component panel and you can see the another panel called properties panel, there you have to change the background color as you like

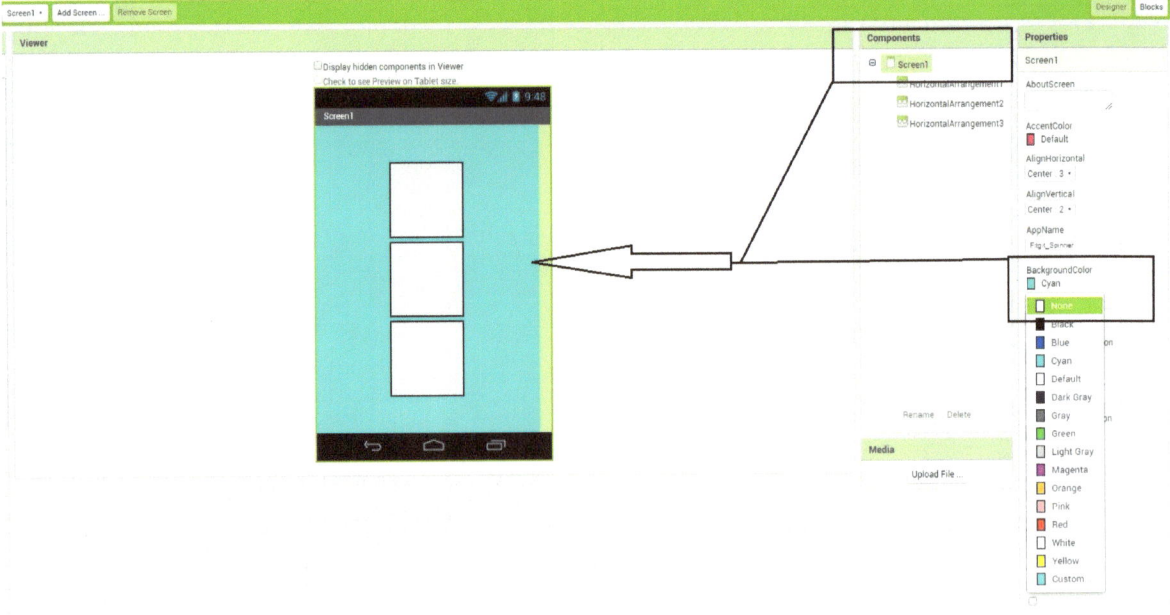

Then open the user interface panel →click and drag **Label** → To first square in the screen1

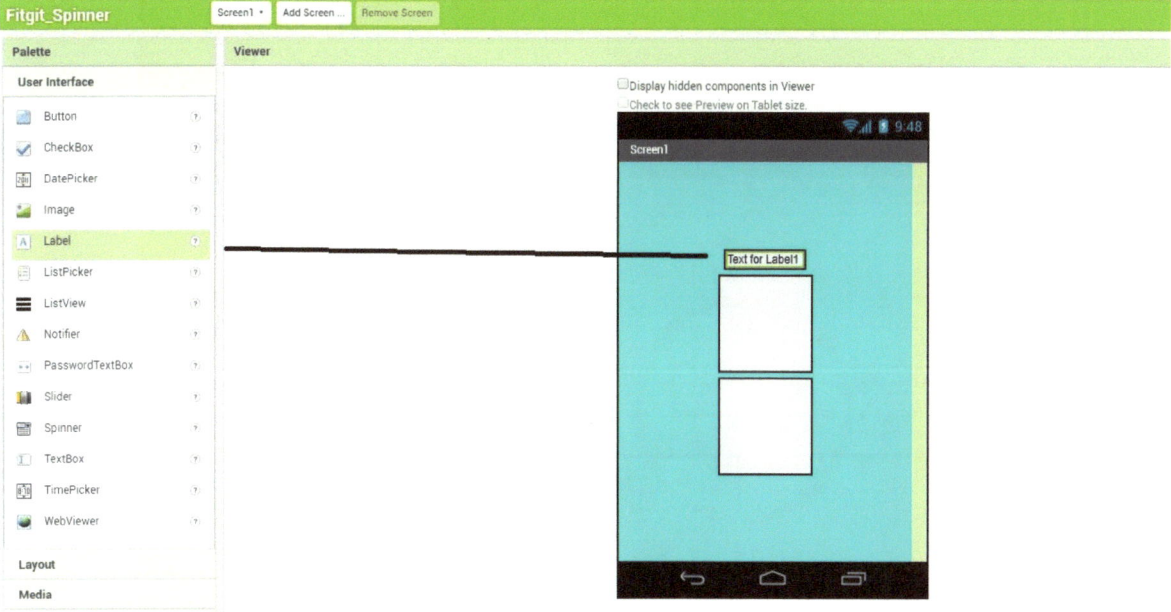

Then select the slider in the same user interface palette

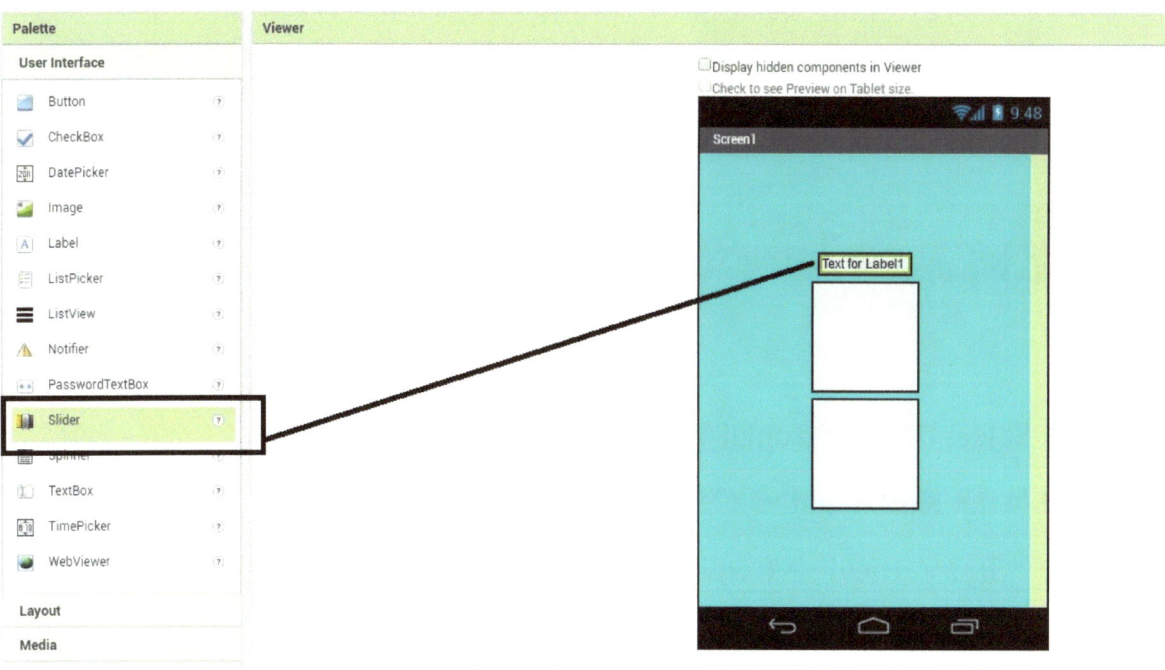

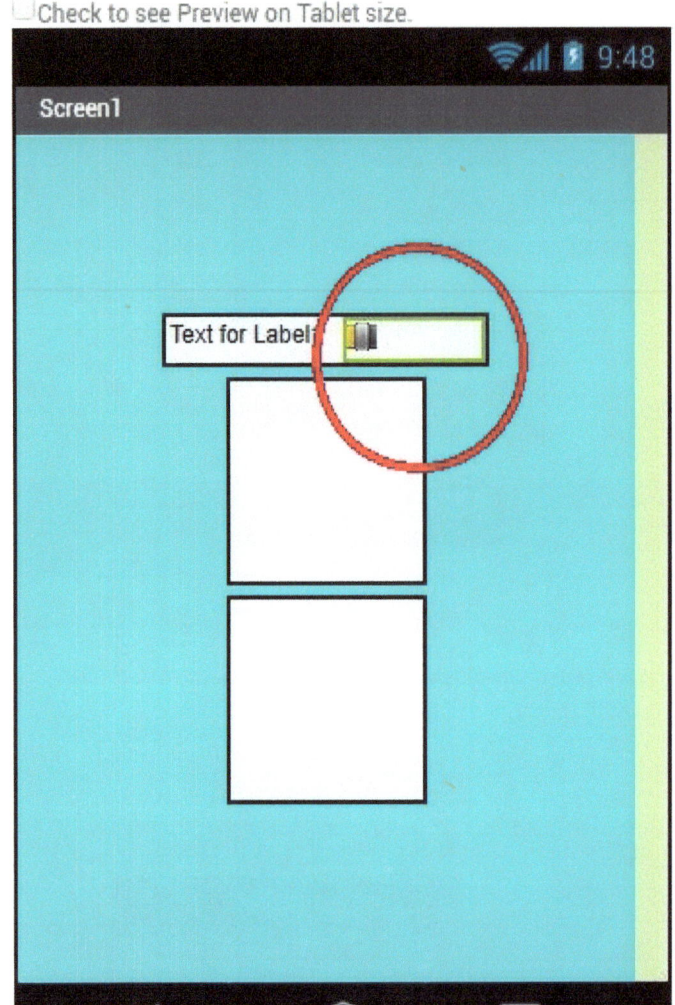

Step1 → Select the HorrizontalArrangement1

Step 2 → AlignHorizontal → Center:3

Step 3 → AlignVertical → Center:2

Step 4 → Height → 10 percent

Step 5 → Width → Fill parent

Now you can see the changes in the screen1 Palette

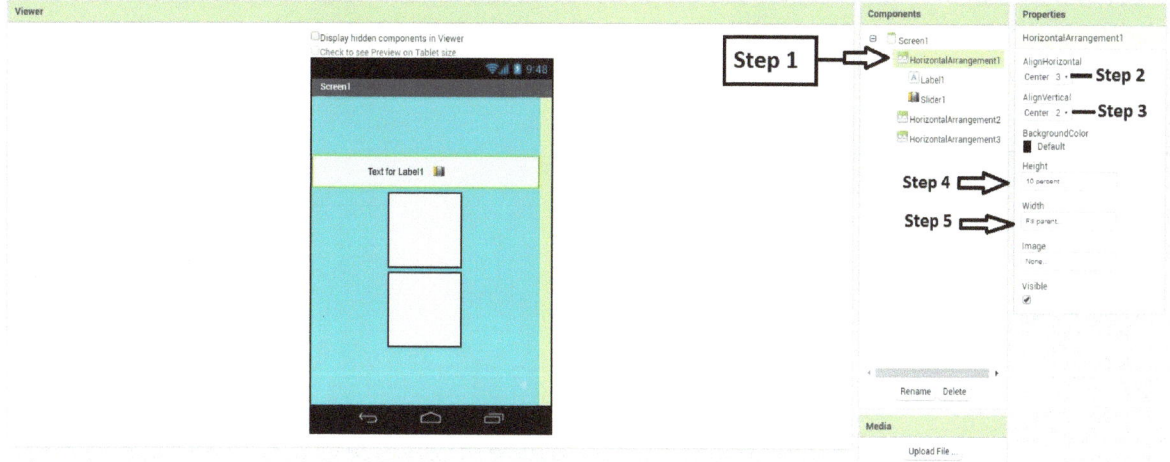

Next,

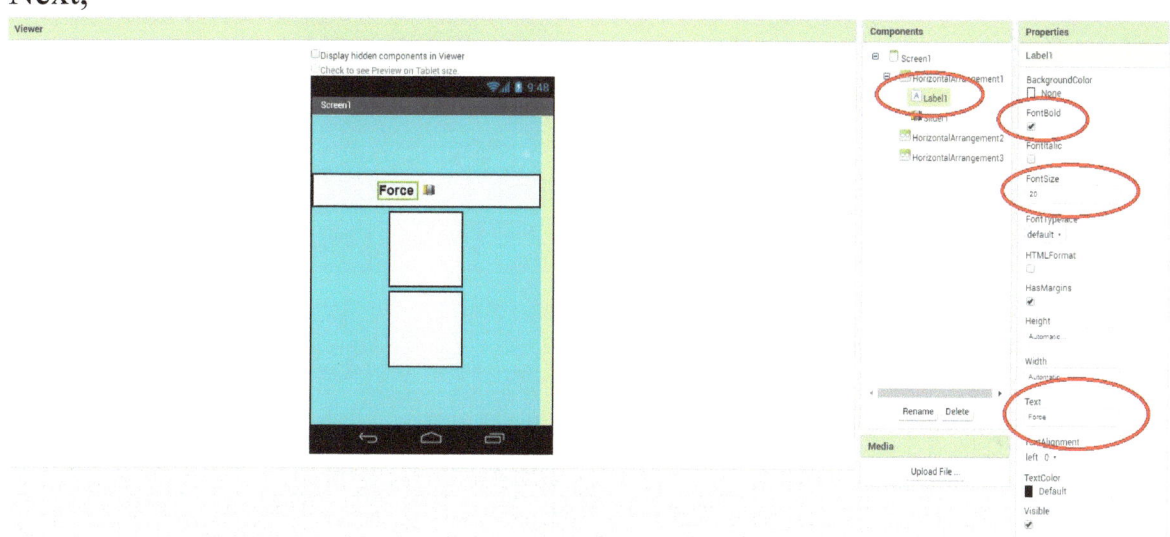

Click Label1 → Properties

→ Tick FontBold

→ FontSize [20]

→ Text Name [Force]

Now, you can see changes in screen1

Then,

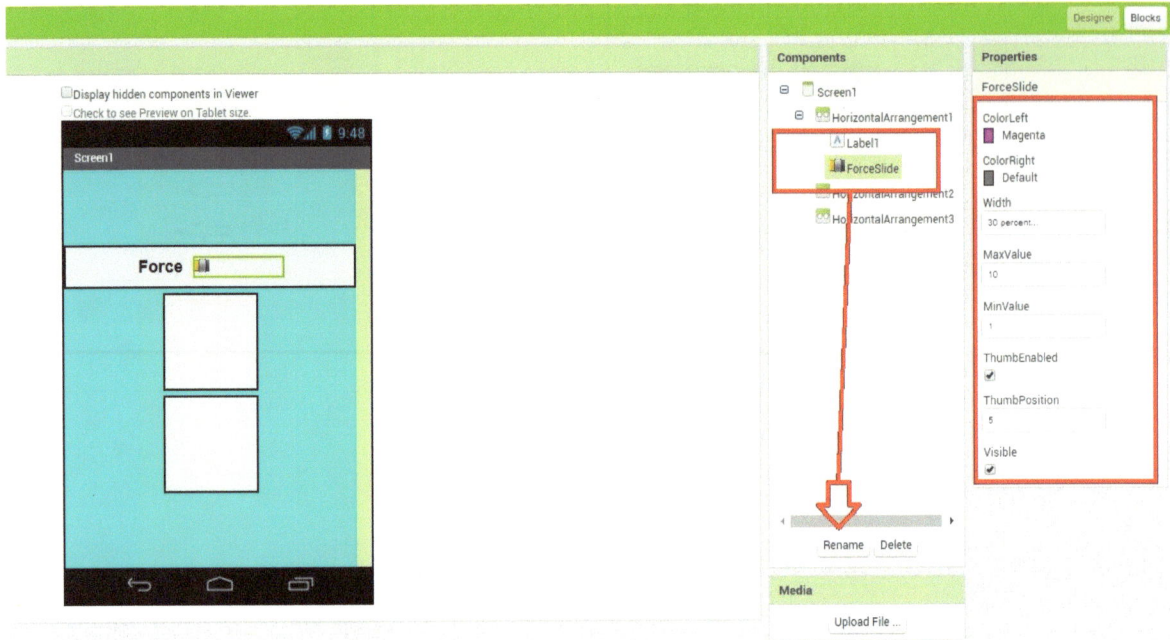

Change the name for slider1 as Forceslider by click Rename and change the Newname…

Change the properties of the Slider as

Colorleft → Magenta (As your like)

Width → 30 percent

Maxvalue → 10

MinValue → 1

Thumb position → 5

Next step, Select the HorizontalArrangement2 in the Component panel or below the Force Slide → Click it

Select → HorizontalArrangement2

Properties → AlignHorizontal → Center : 3

AlignVertical → Center : 2

Height → 10 percent

Width → Fill Parent

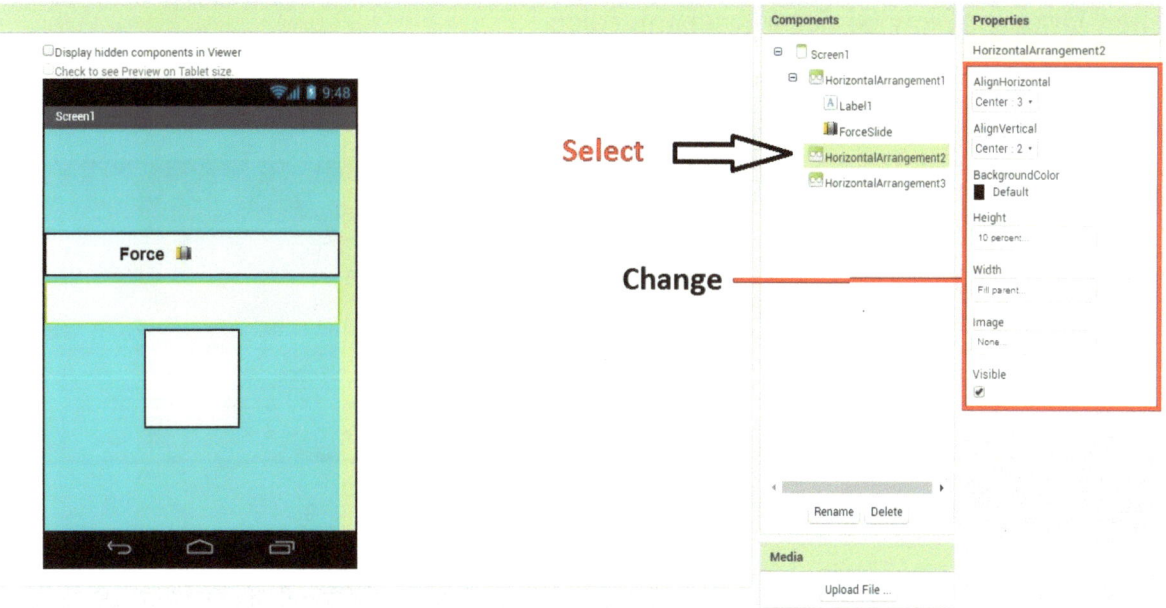

Then, pick a new label from user interface palette

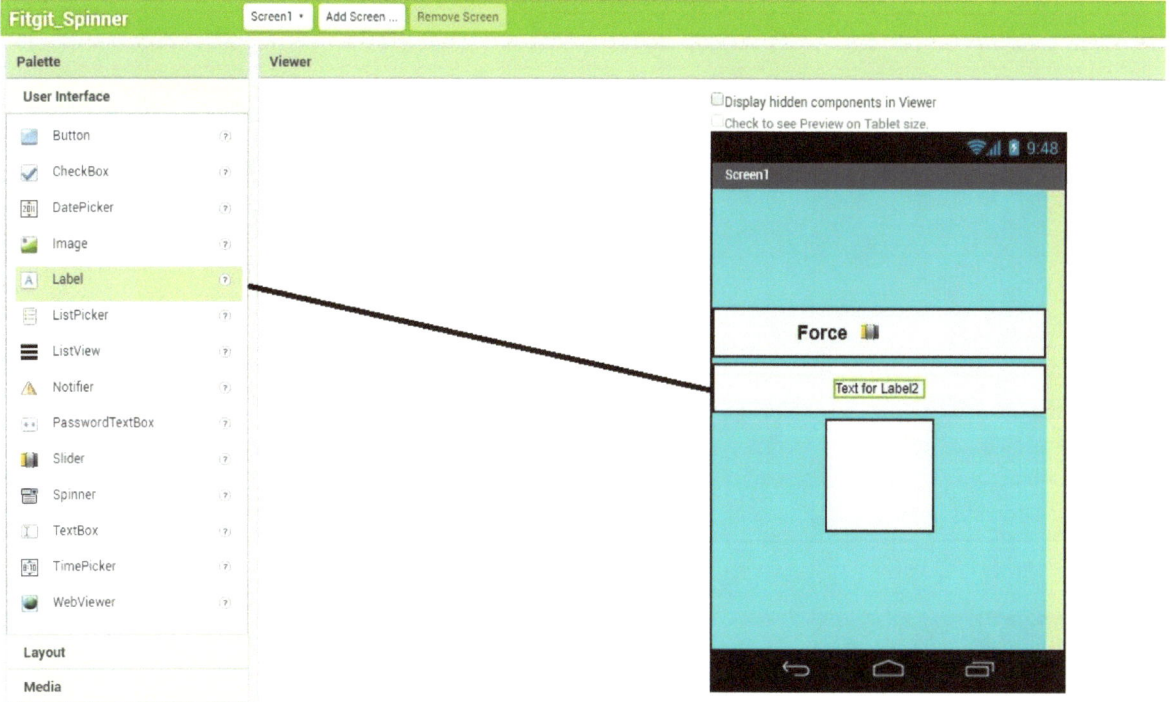

Drag label to the HorizontalArrangement2 (Second Square box)

Then Drag the New Slider in user interface

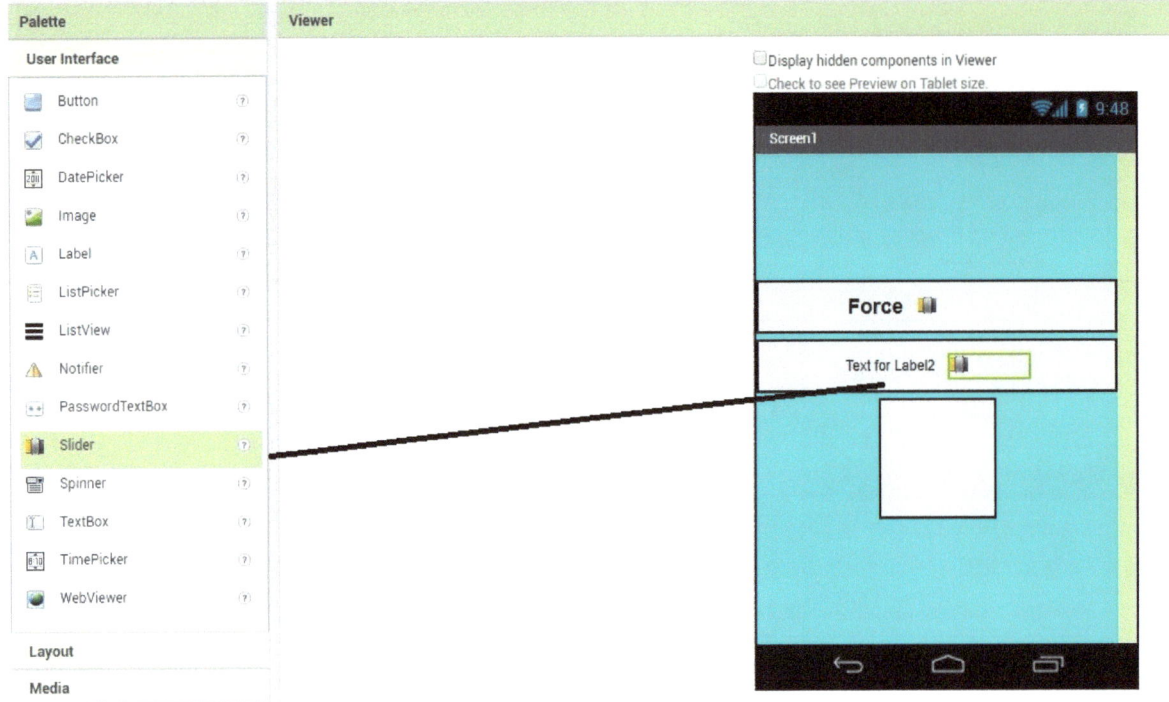

Then Click Label2 → Make these Changes

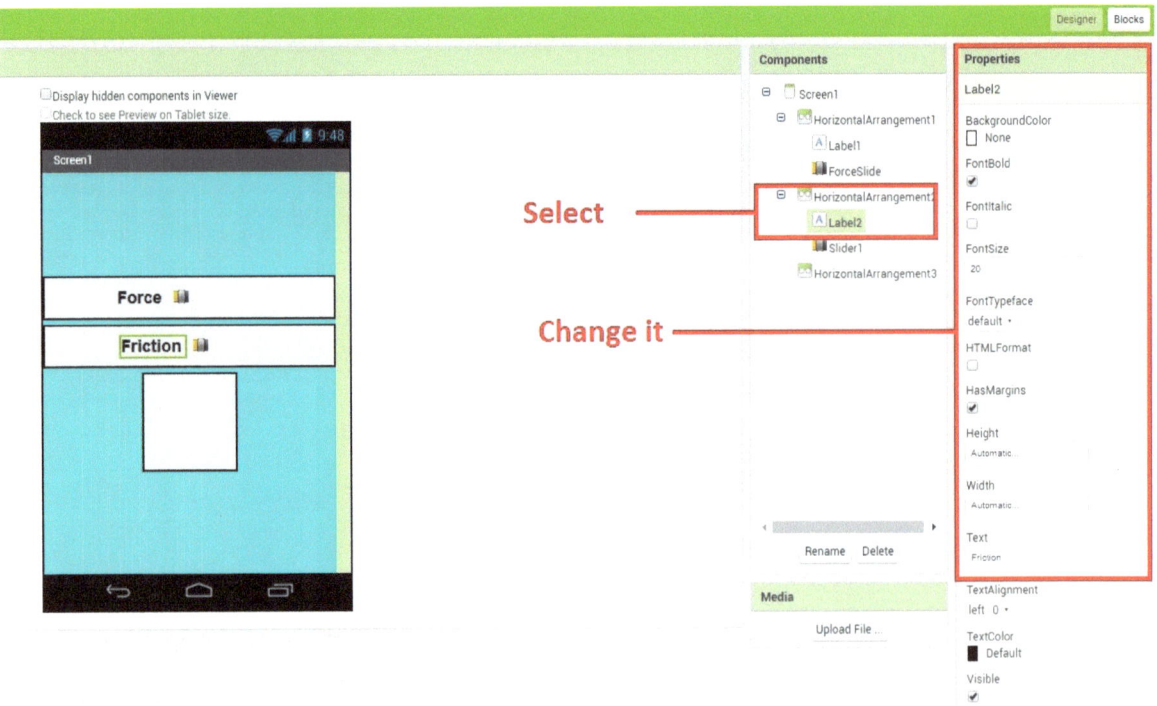

Label2 → Properties

→ FontBold (Tick)

Fontsize → 20

Text → Friction

Then you have to move slider1,

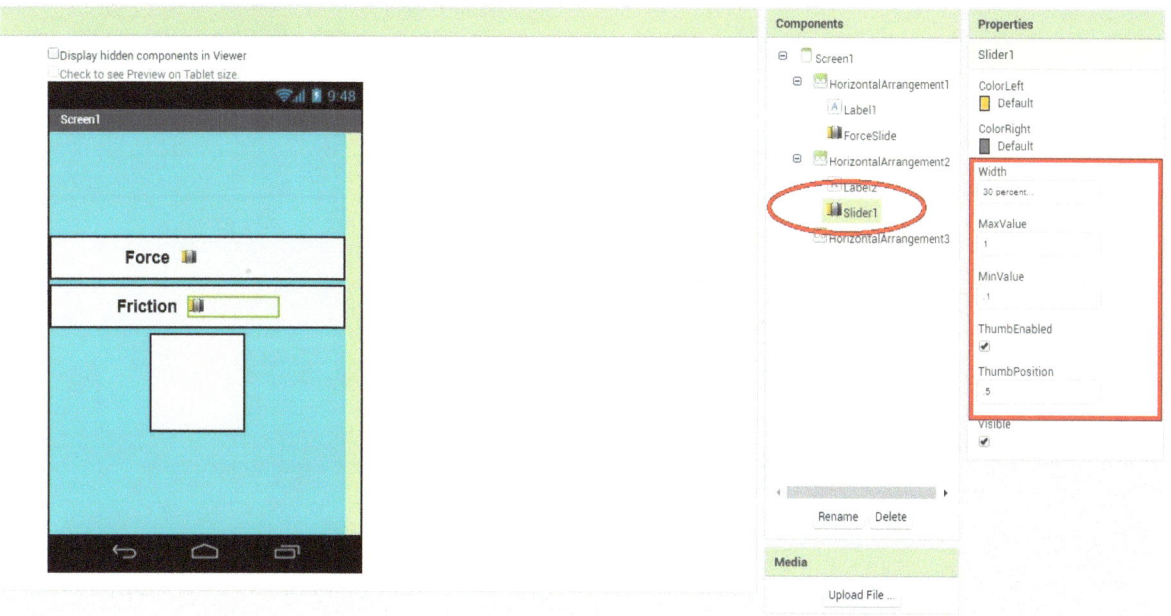

Slider1 → Properties

→ width (30 percent)

→ Max value (1)

→ Min Value (0.1)

→ ThumbPosition (5)

And change the name for the Slider1 as → FrictionSlide

Then,

In the palette, Select the DRAWING AND ANIMATION – From that select

Canvas → Drag the Canvas to → HorizontalArrangement3

Then there was a change in the Square (Horizontal Arrangement3)

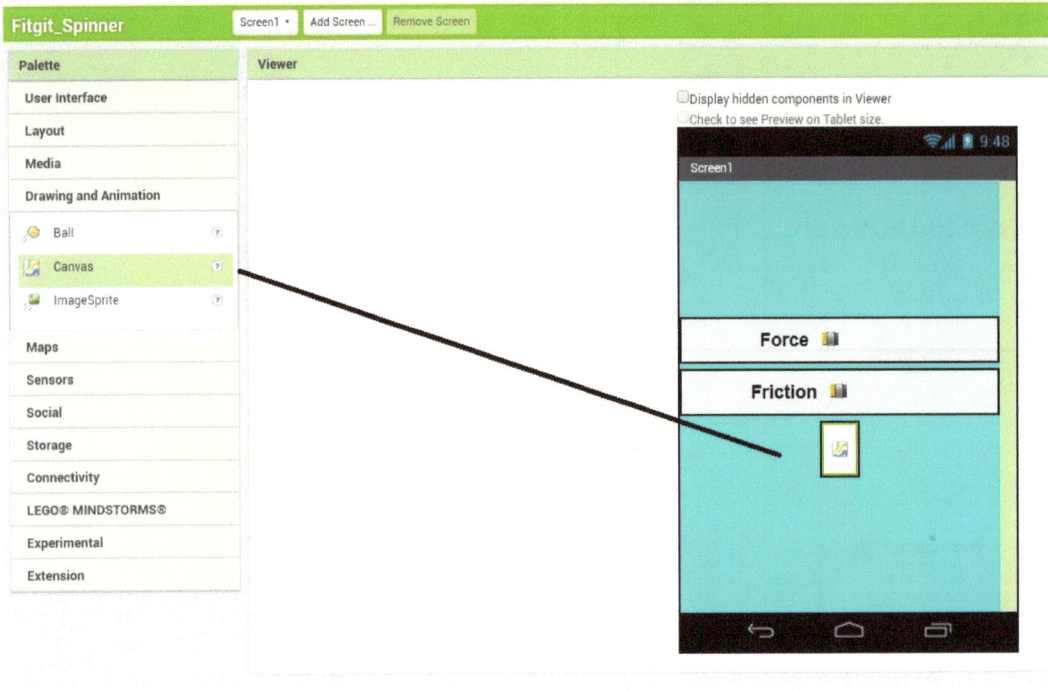

Then Select Canvas → Canvas properties

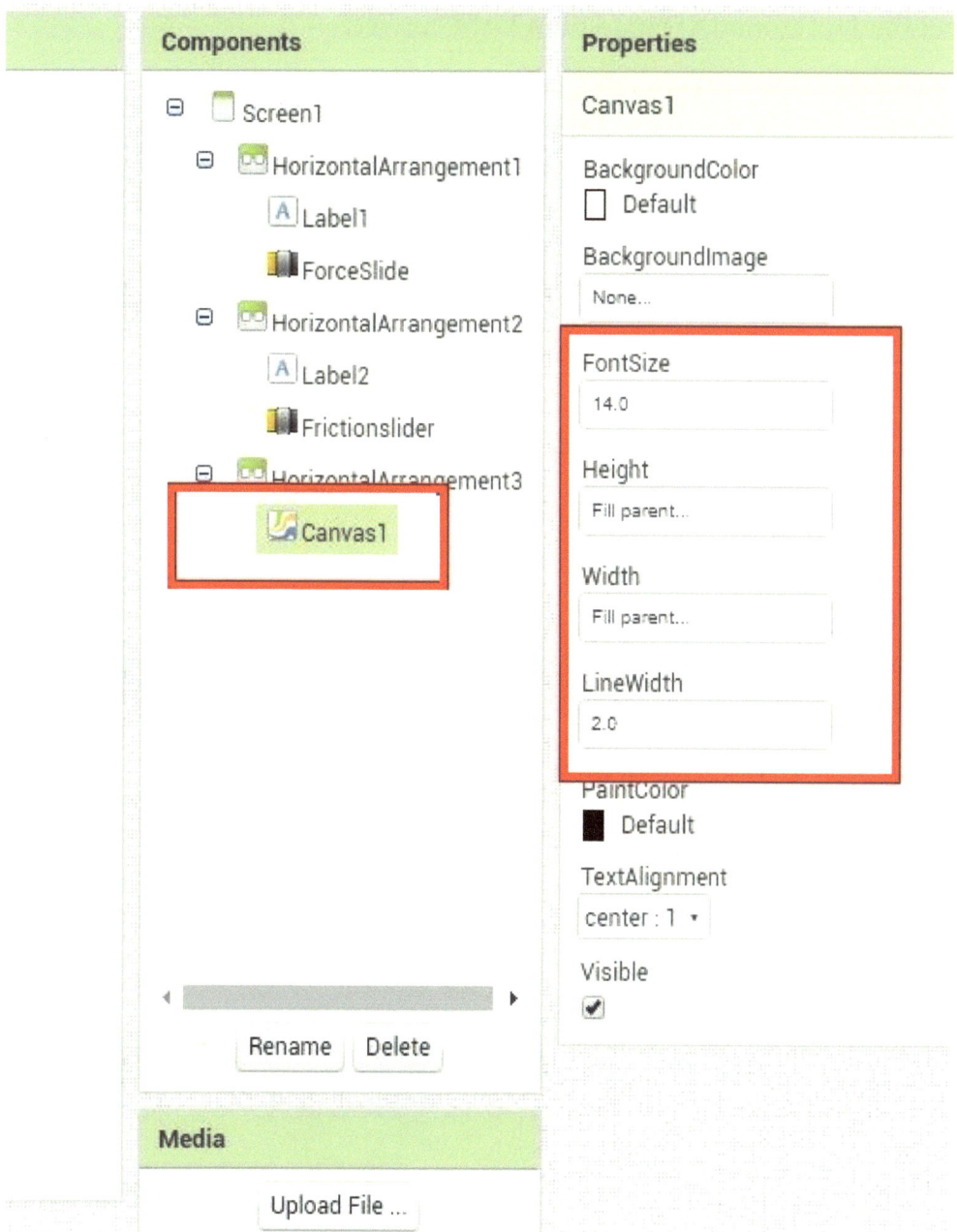

Canvas1 → Properties

→ Font size [14.0]

→ Height [Fill Parent]

→ Width [Fill Parent]

→ Line Width [2.0]

After that select the HorizontalArrangement3 of Canvas1

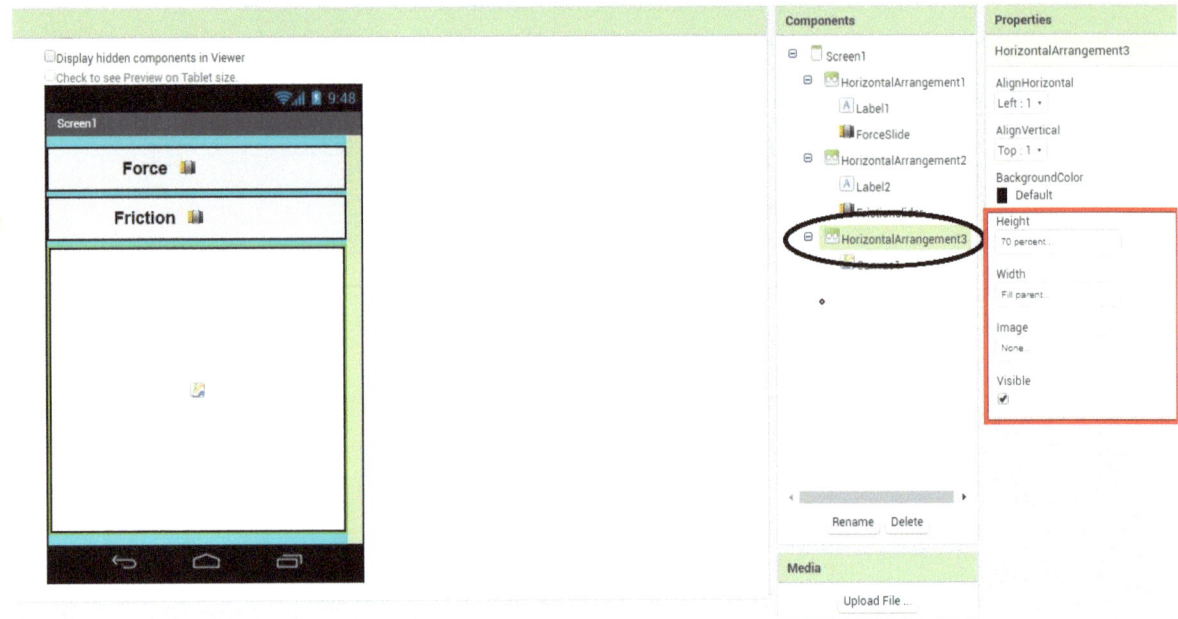

HorizontalArrangement3 → Properties

→ Height [70 percent]

→ Width [Fill parent]

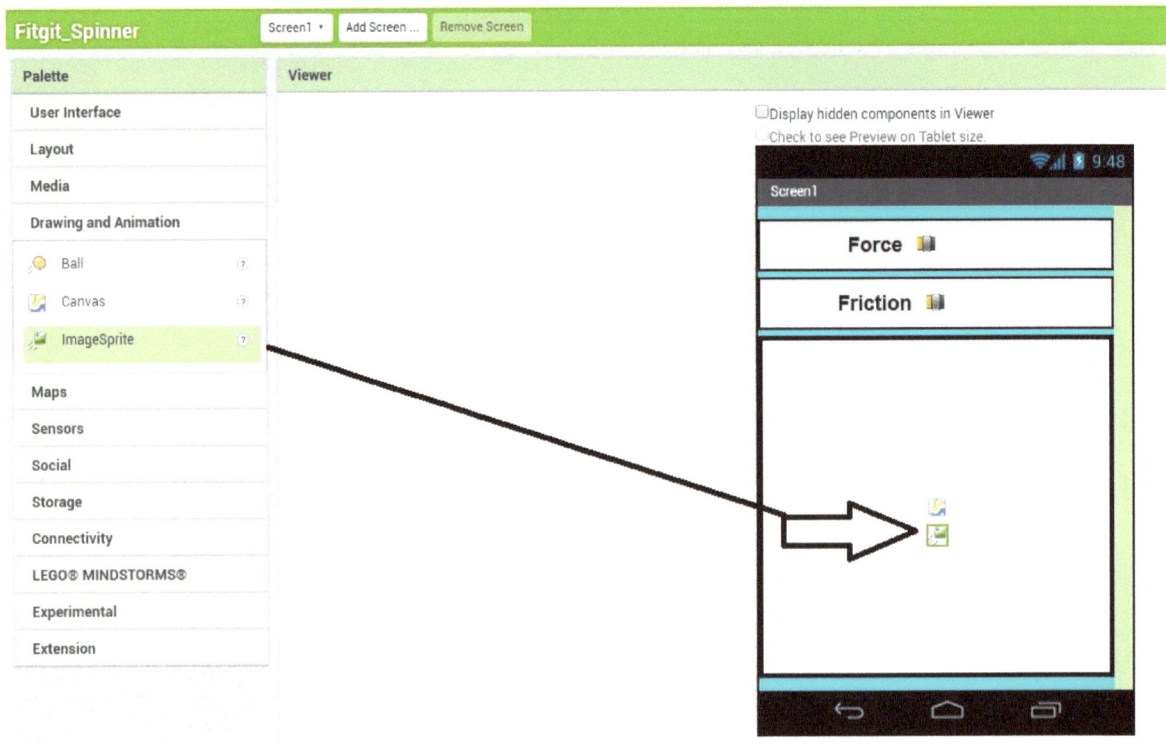

In palette panel, user can see the Drawing and animation division below the Media, where you have to select the ImageSprite

Drag the Imagesprite to the HorizontalArrangement3 or Canvas layout

Next, you have to upload a Fitget Spinner Image to the Imagesprite

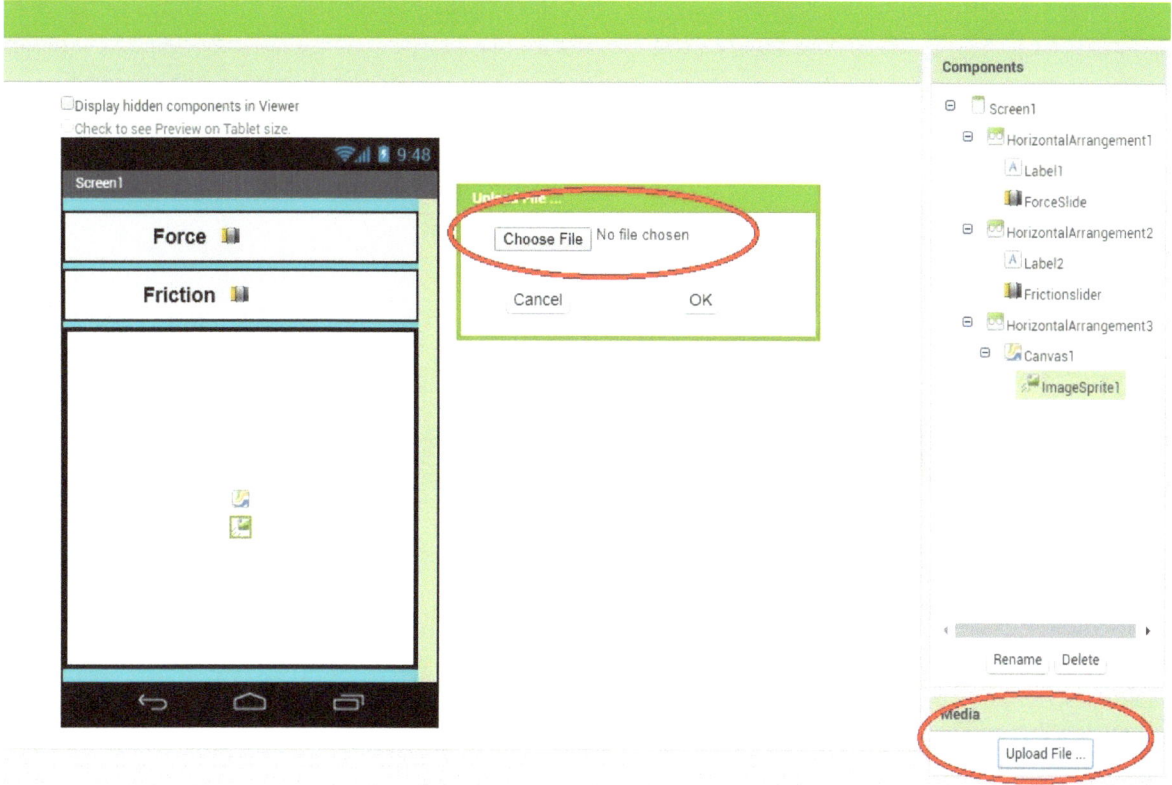

For Fitget Spinner Image Go to Browser and type Fitget spinner PNG ,,,,,

There you can get lot of varieties,,

Note: For this App only PNG image is Applicable

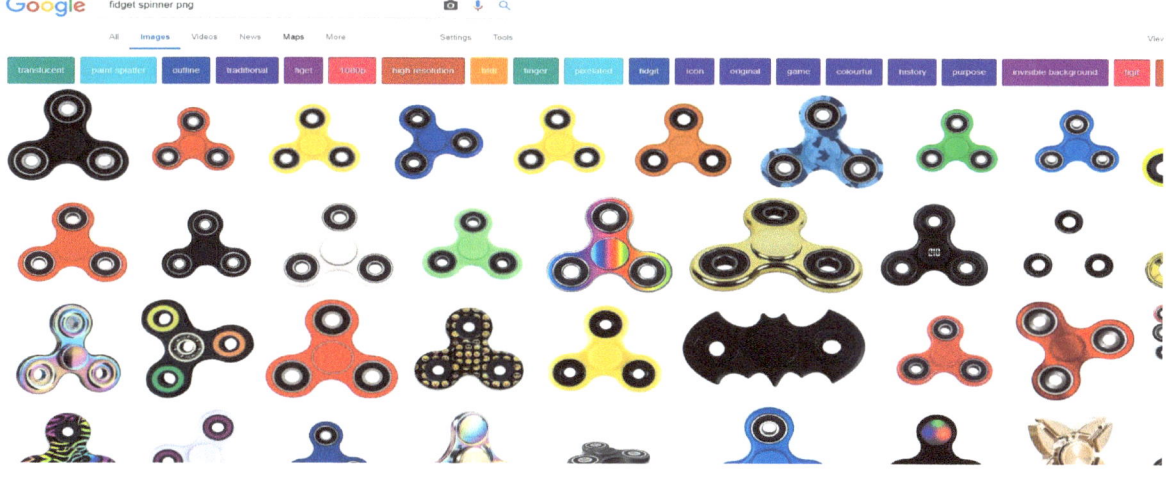

Change the picture as you have uploaded file (eg.Figit.png) and Click ok

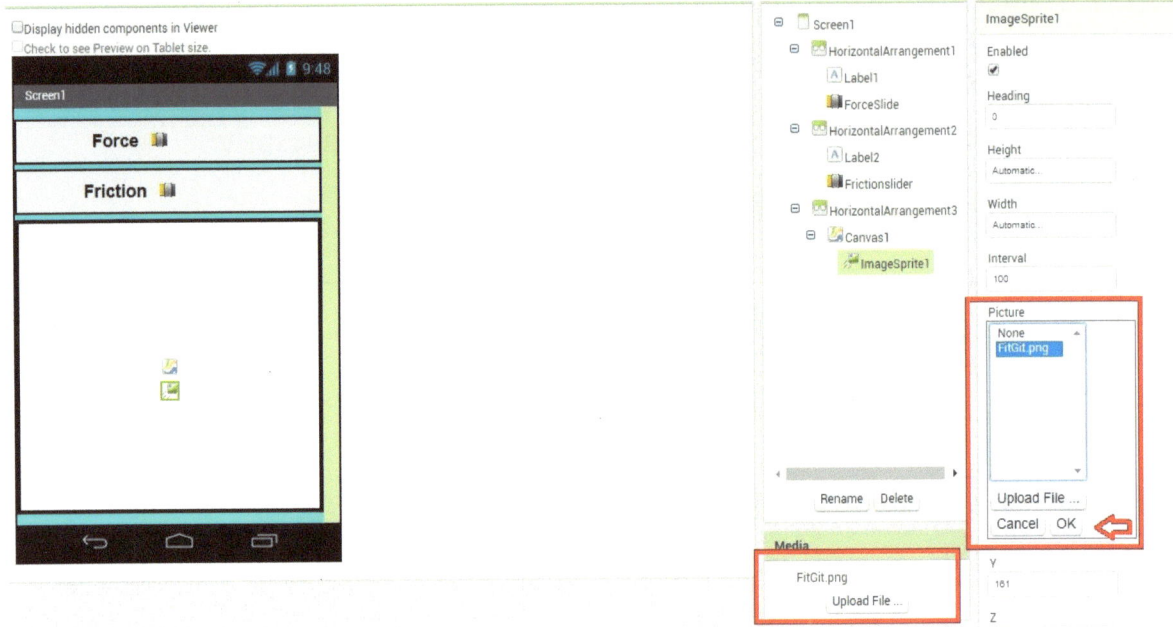

If the image beyond the screen, not at a matter. We will fix that in the Blocks

Next you have to do, Change the name of Image spirit as FitgetSpinner

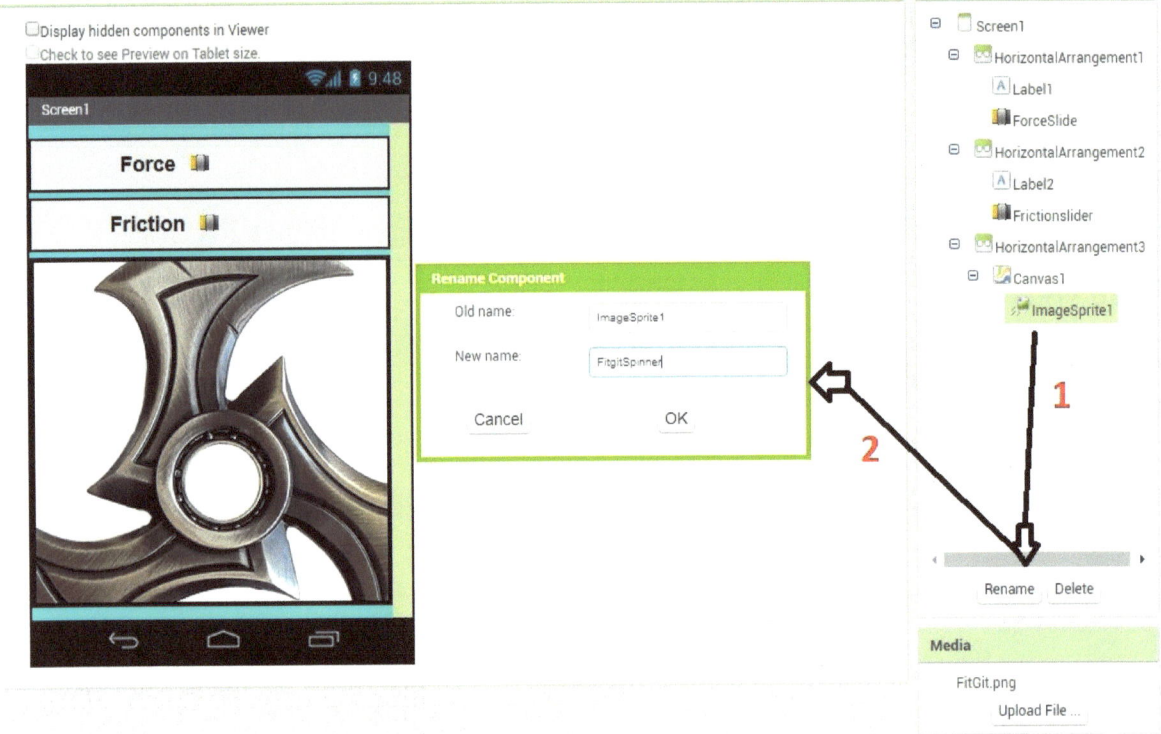

After that you have to Change the specification of the FitgetSpinner

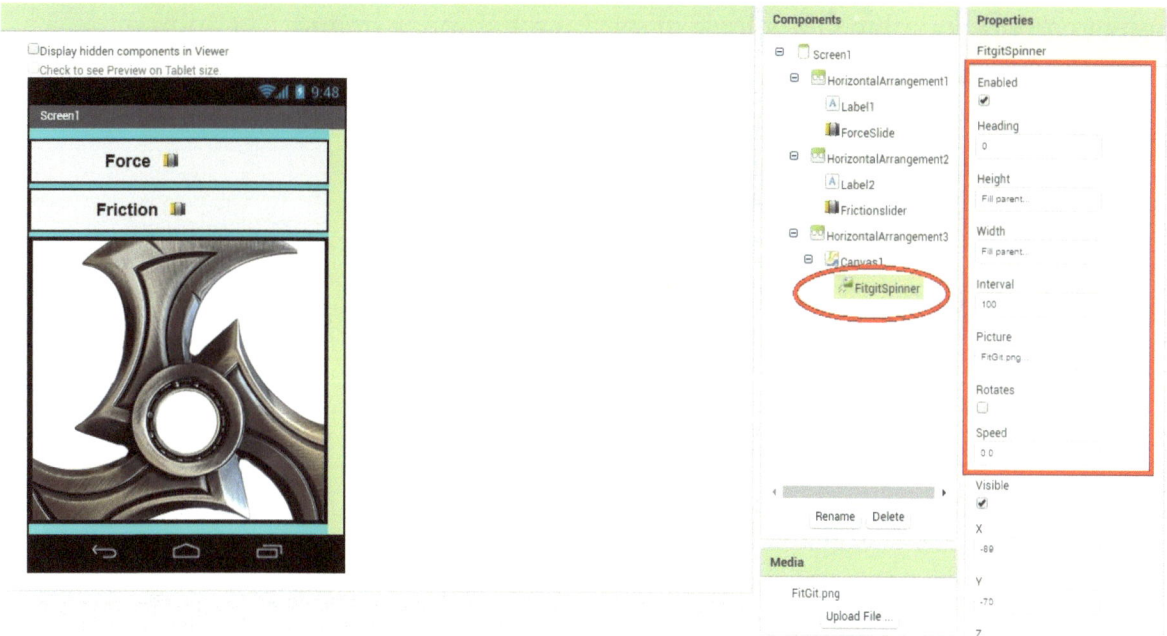

Components → FitgetSpinner → Properties

Height → FillParent

Width → Fillparent

Rotate → Remove Tick

Then Select the Friction slider and change the color which is in the properties

Default color is yellow, user can change the color as like as, but we choose Red for our conveniences.

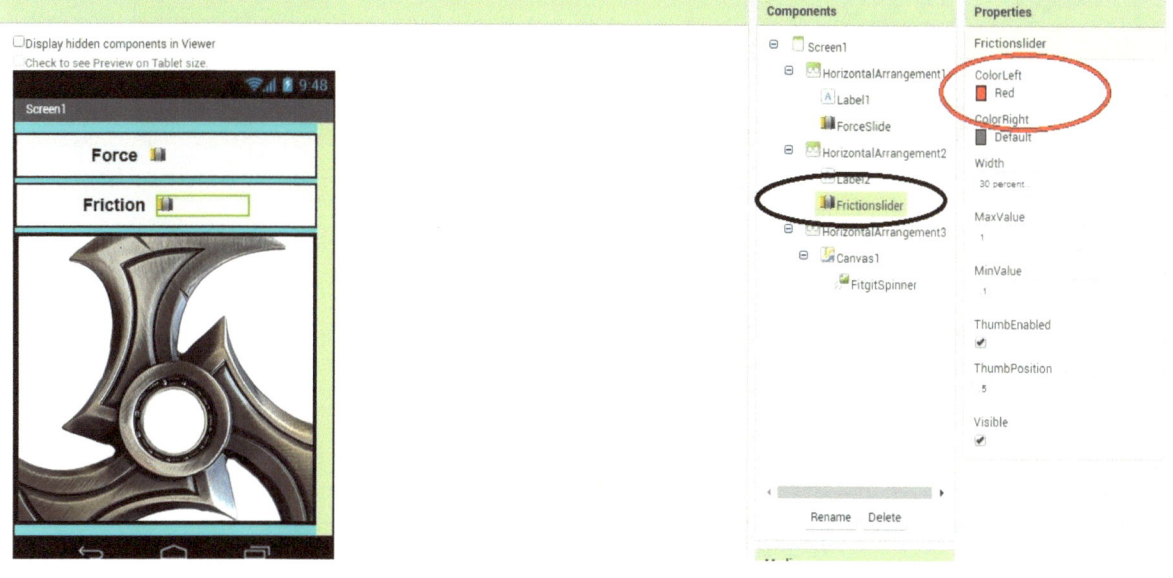

Select canvas and place the clock in the Fitget spinner image ... Clock is located in the sensor section.

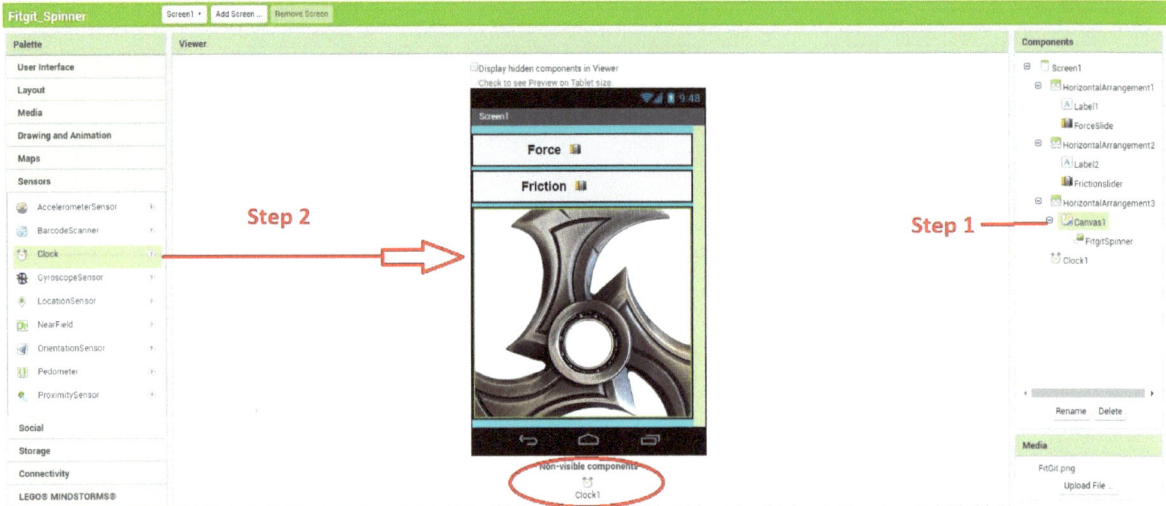

Make the clock Time interval to 1000 to 10

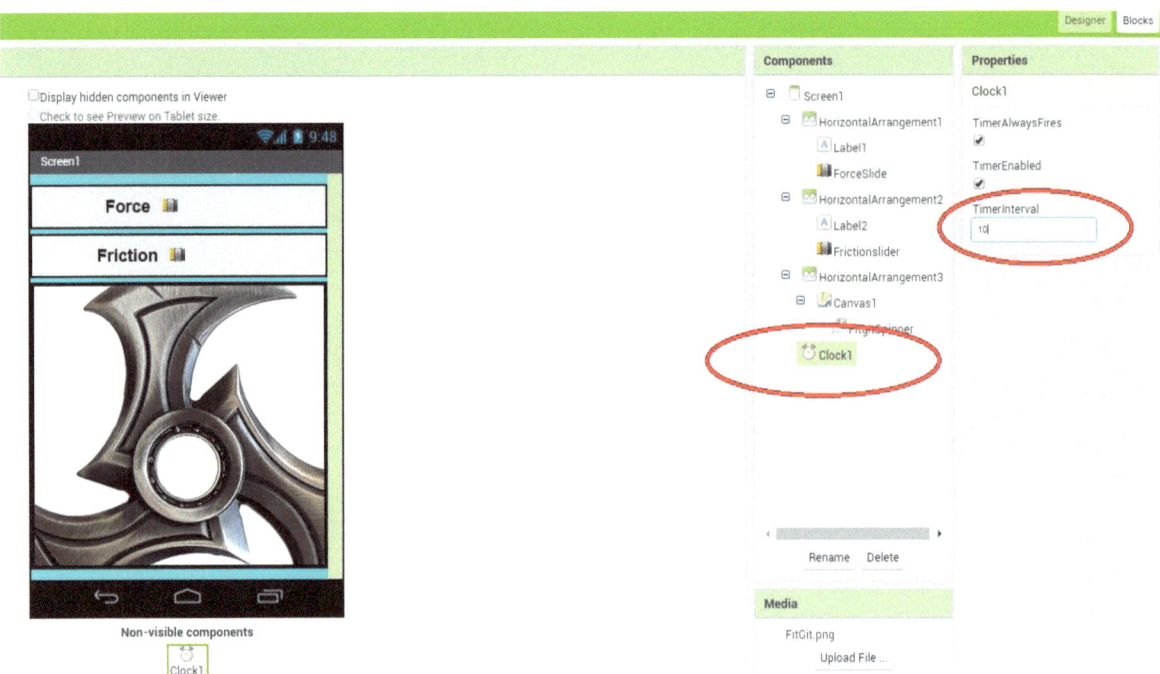

Here we completed the Designer Section, we have to move Block side, which was the backend section of this Application.

Now you have to follow the Logics which are selected in the Blocks panel which Is located left side

Step 1:

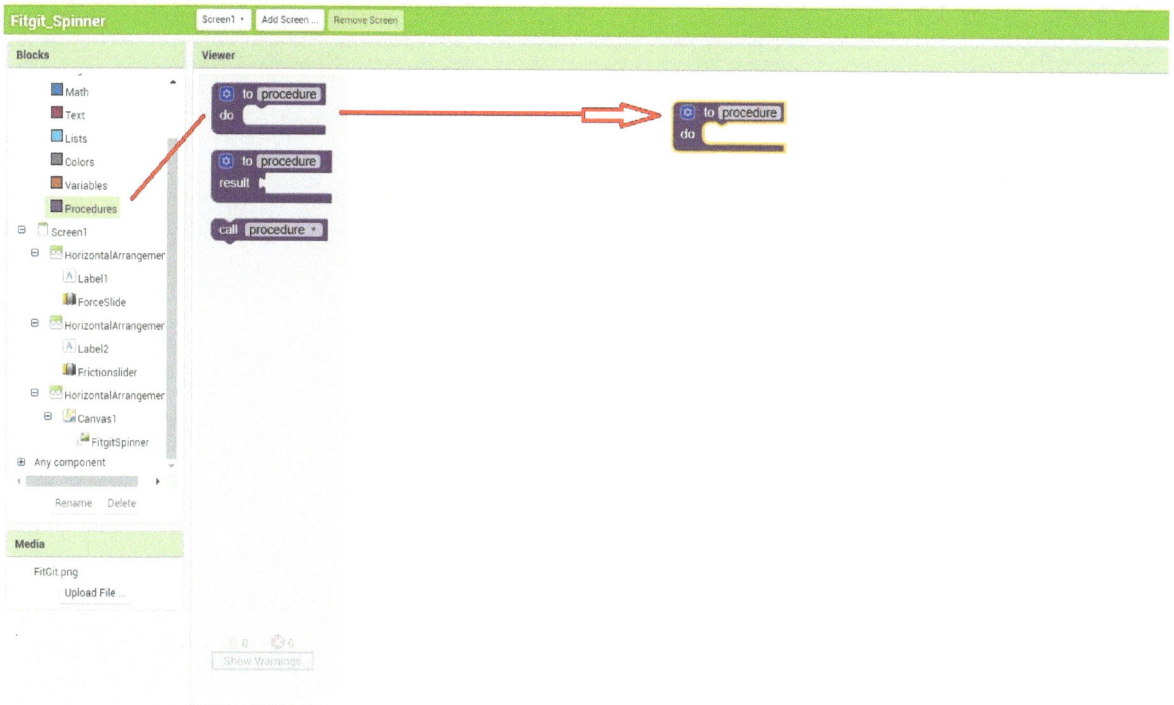

Step 2:

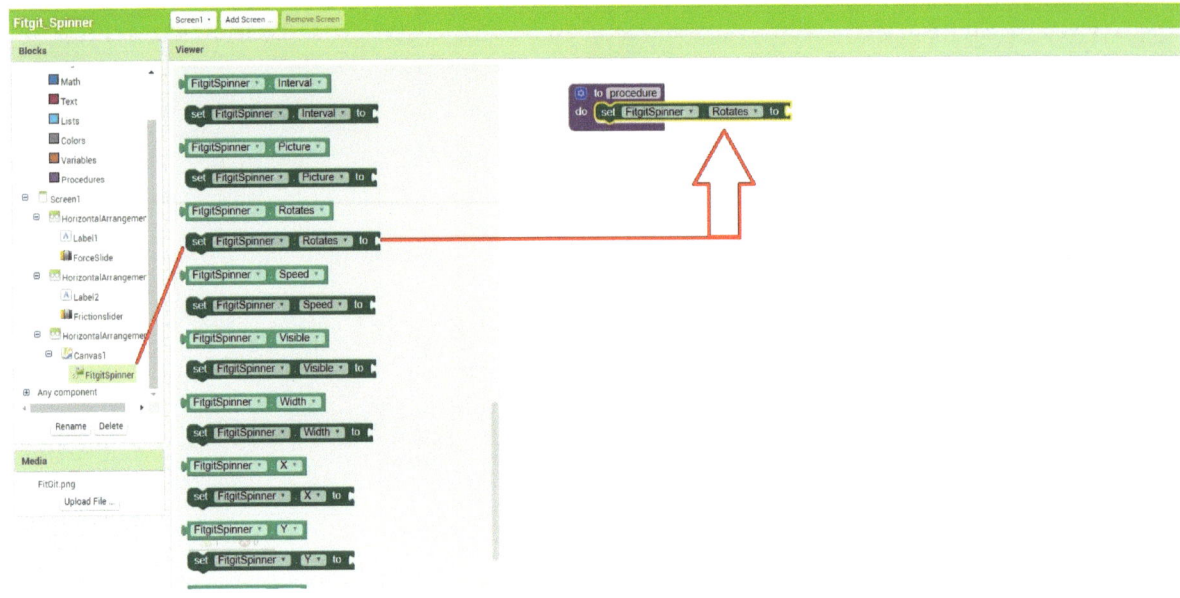

Step 3:

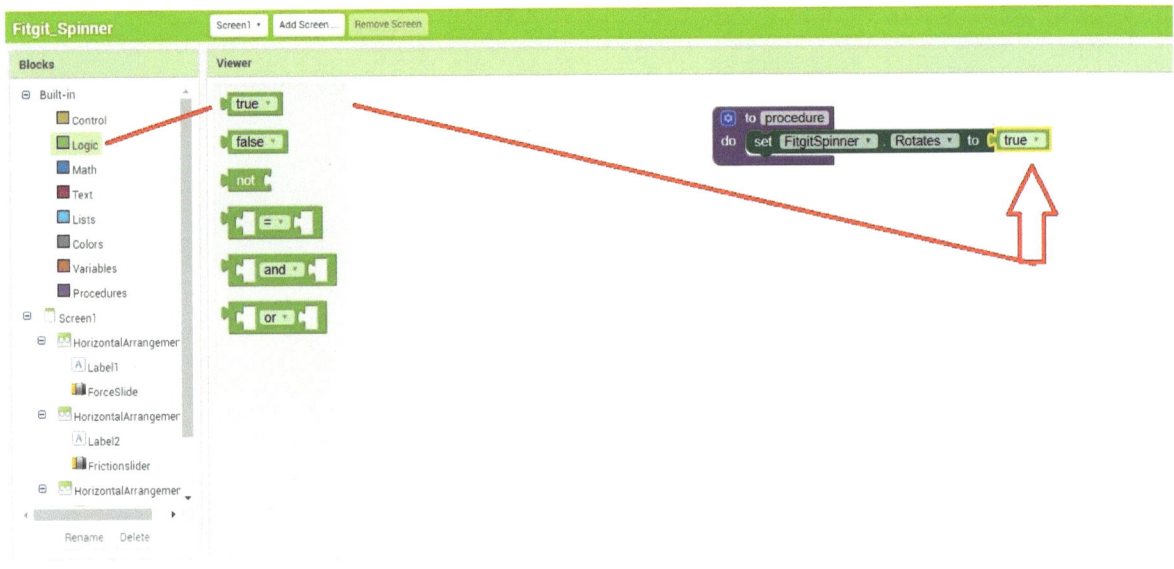

Step 4:

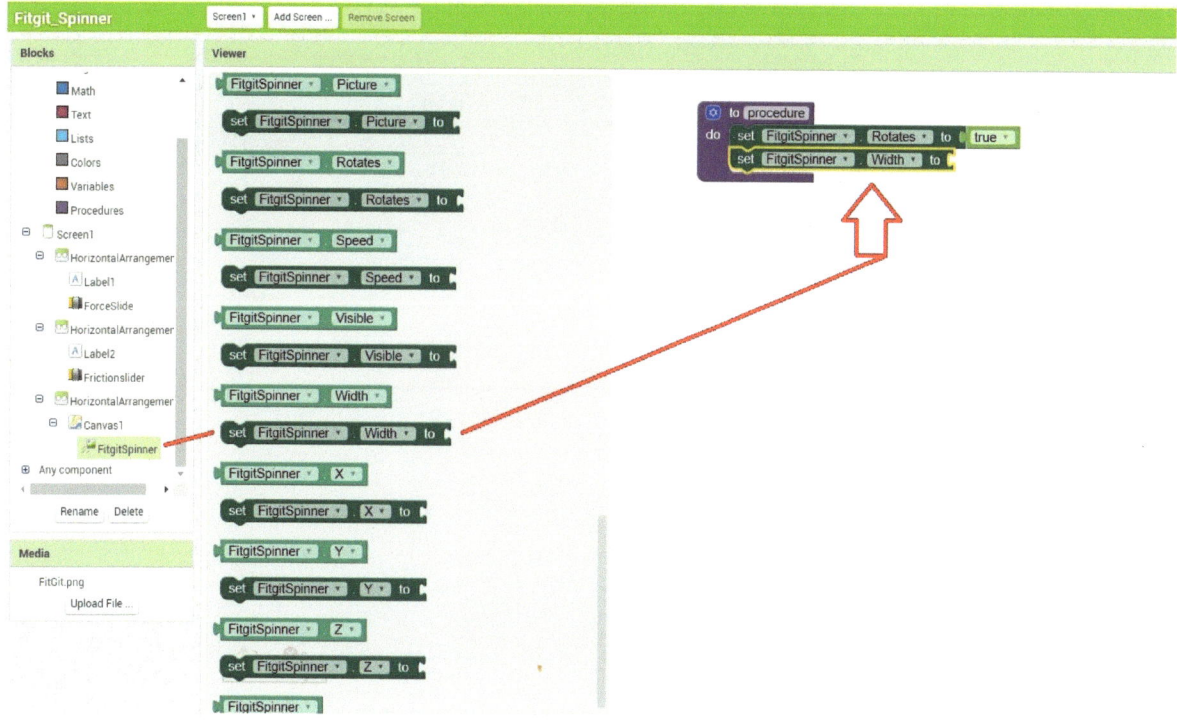

Step 5:

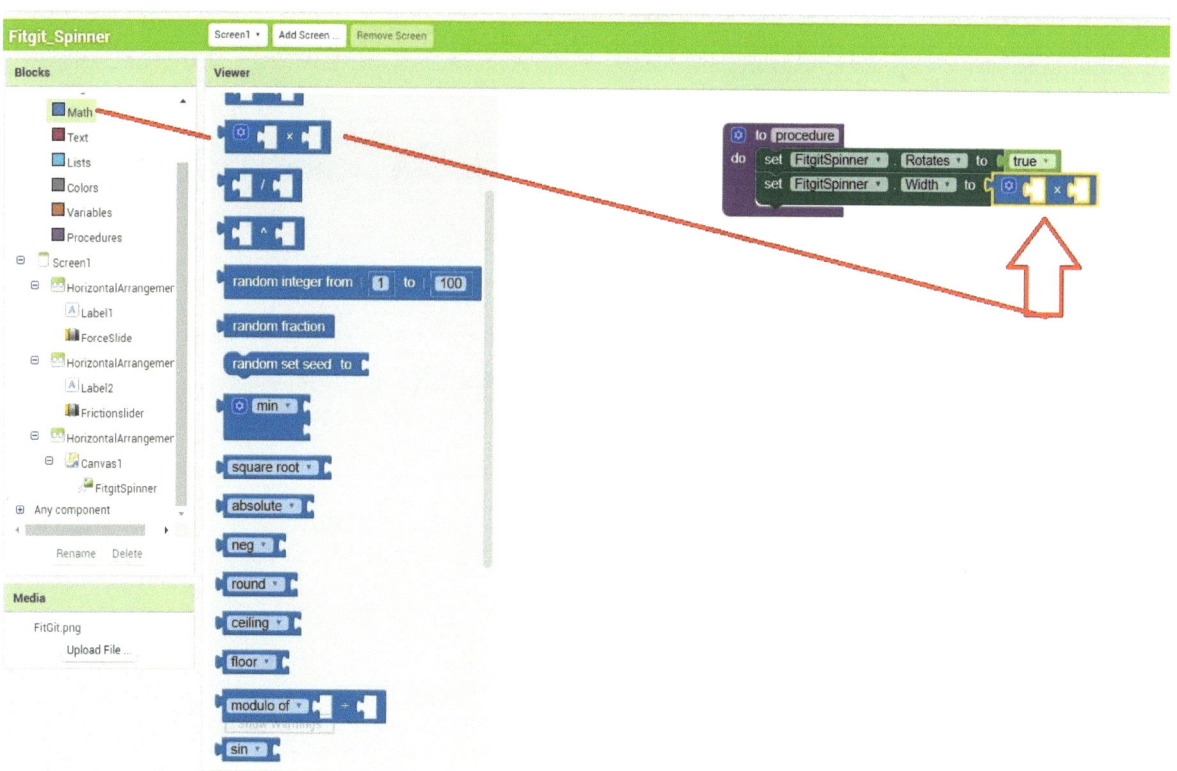

Step 6:

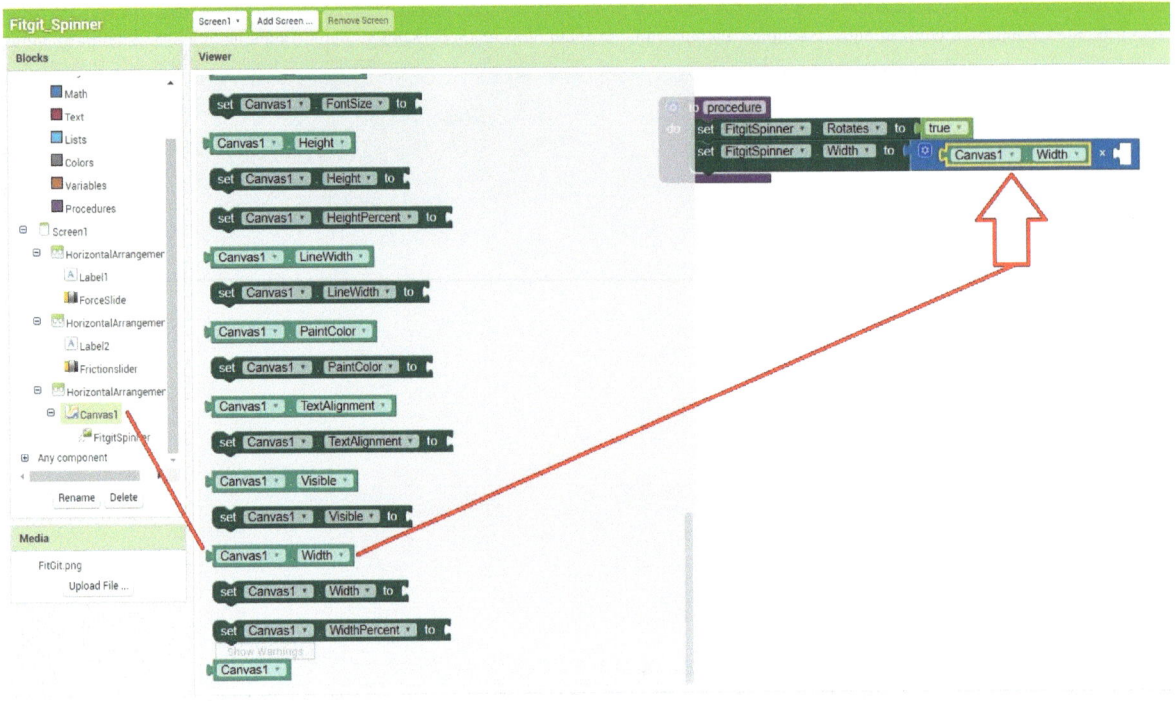

Steps 7:

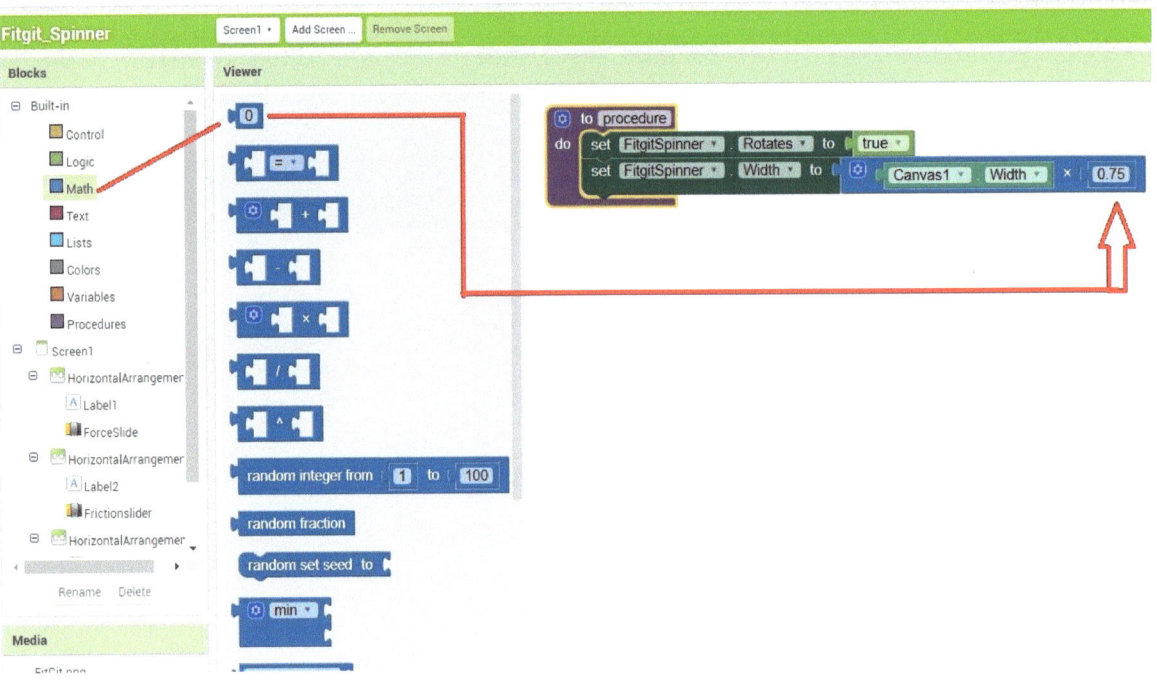

Step 8:

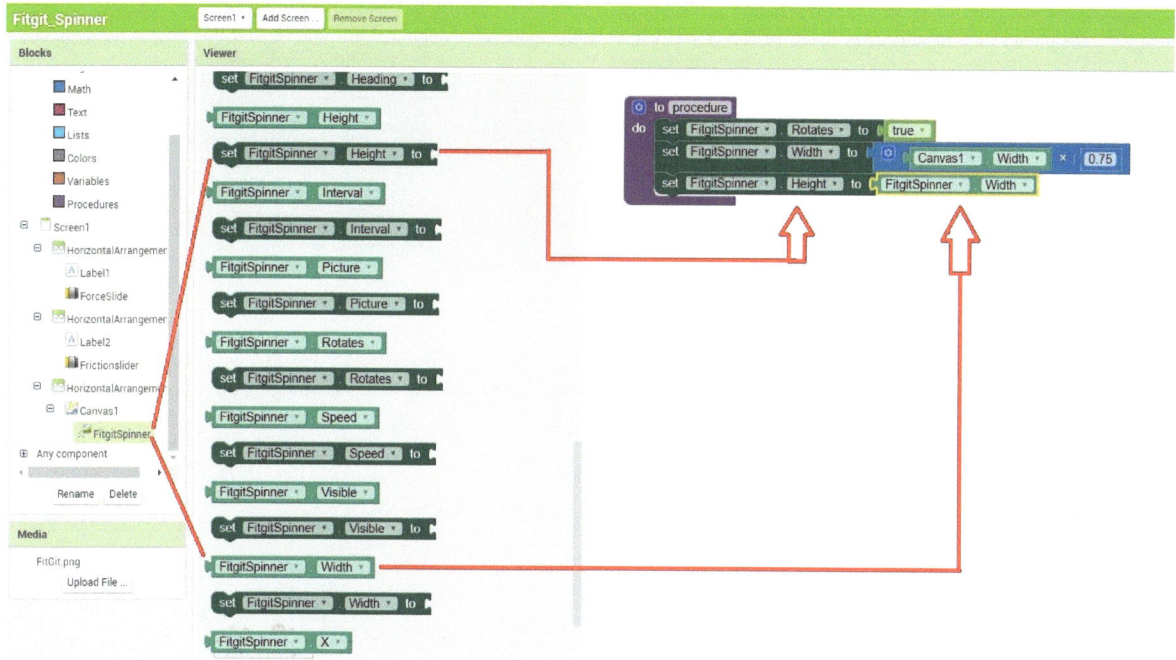

Step 9:

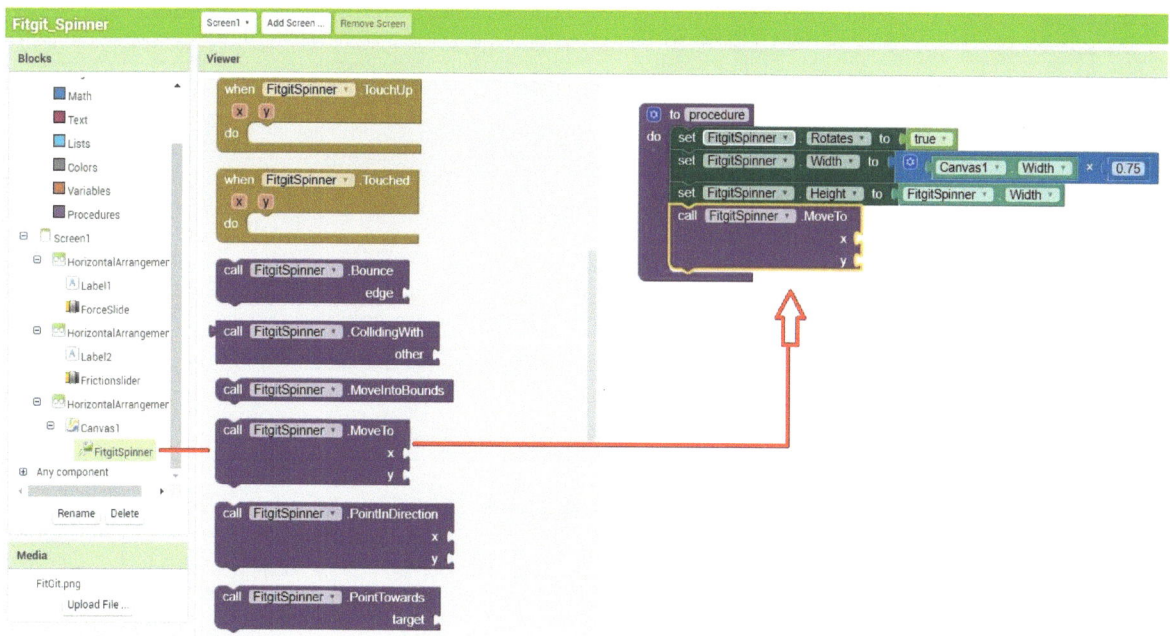

Step 10:

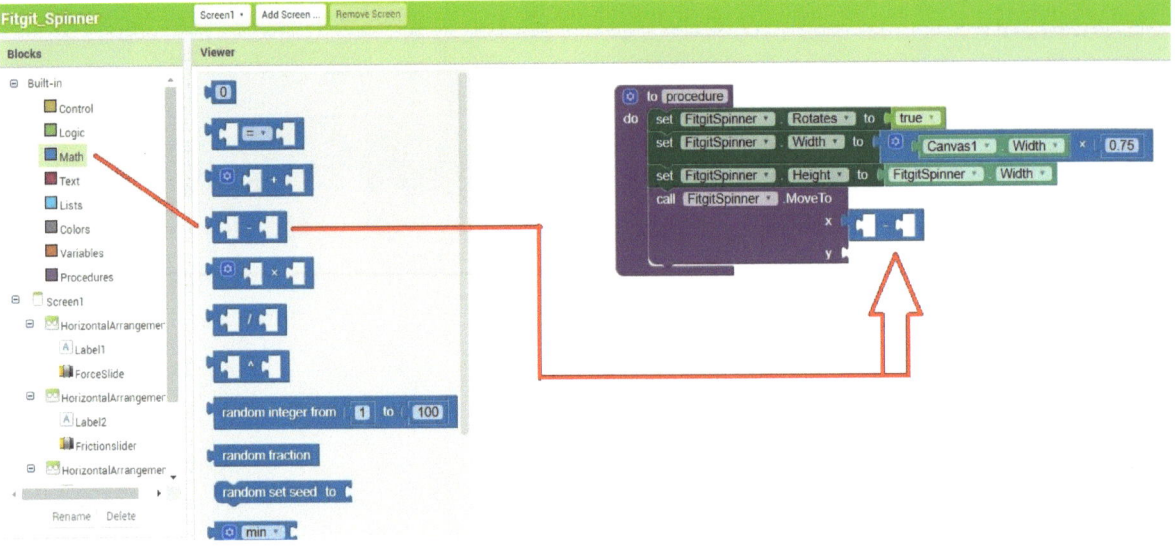

Step 11:

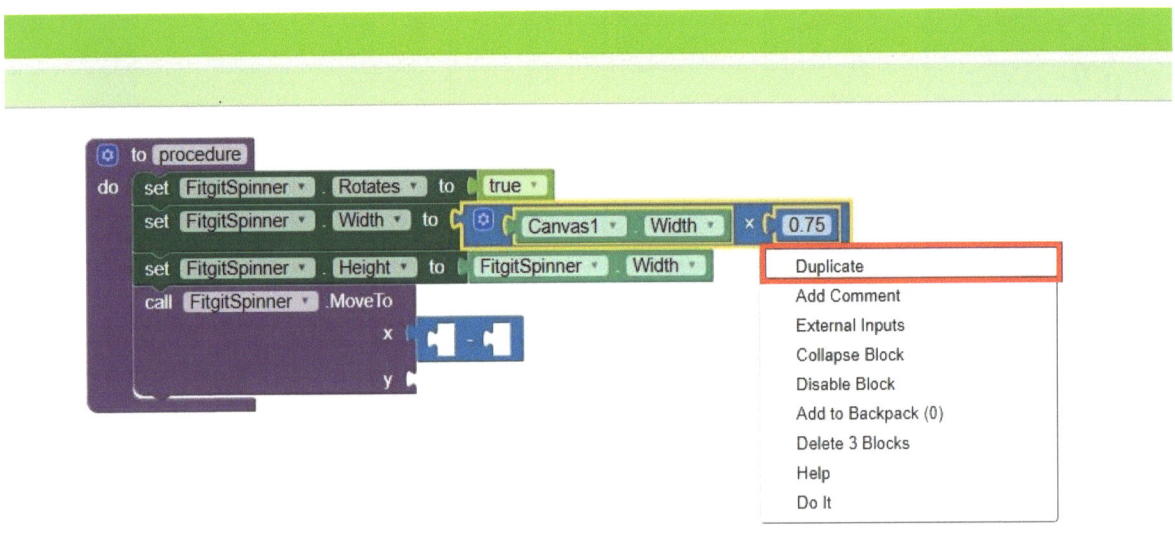

After Duplicate, you can get same block again. Make Four Duplicate box and change the 0.75 value to 0.5 as mentioned below figure

Step 11.1:

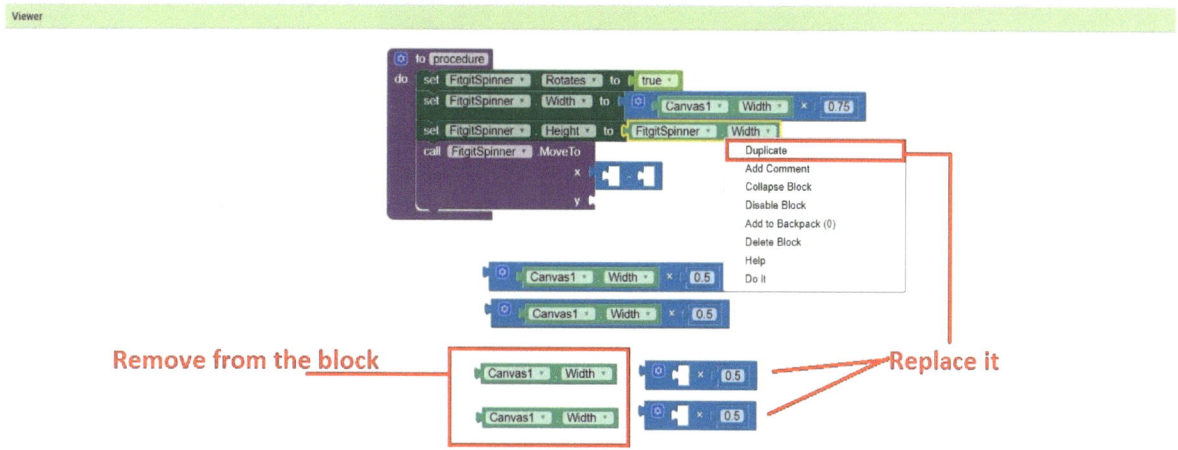

Step 11.2:

Step 12:

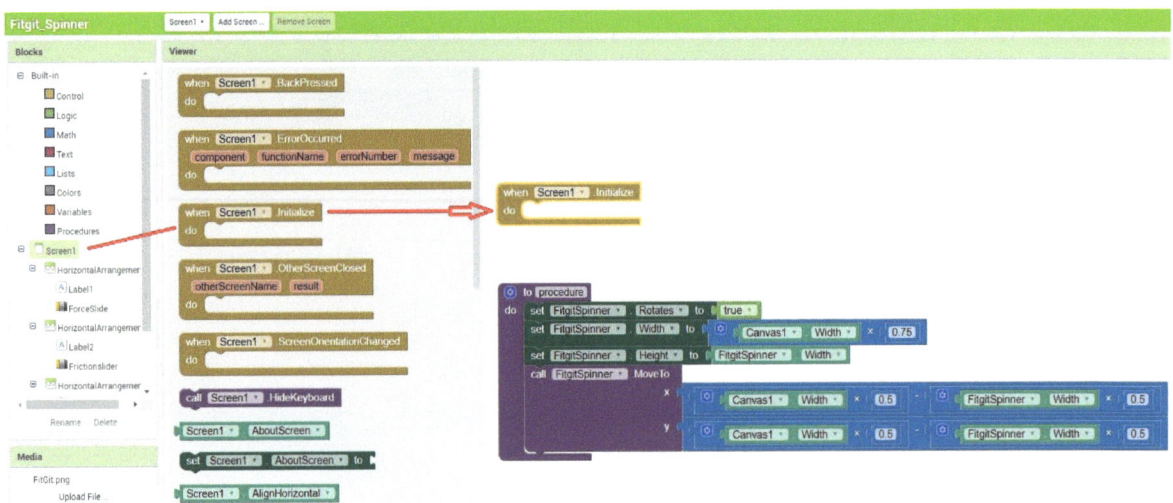

Step 13:

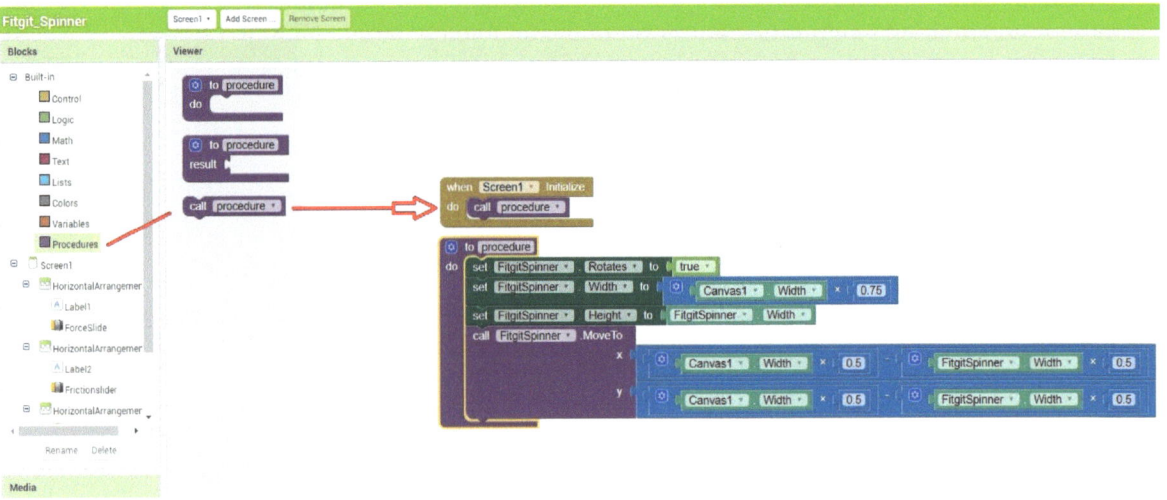

Step 14:

Initialize three variable Names

- ➔ Rotation
- ➔ Friction
- ➔ Rotation speed

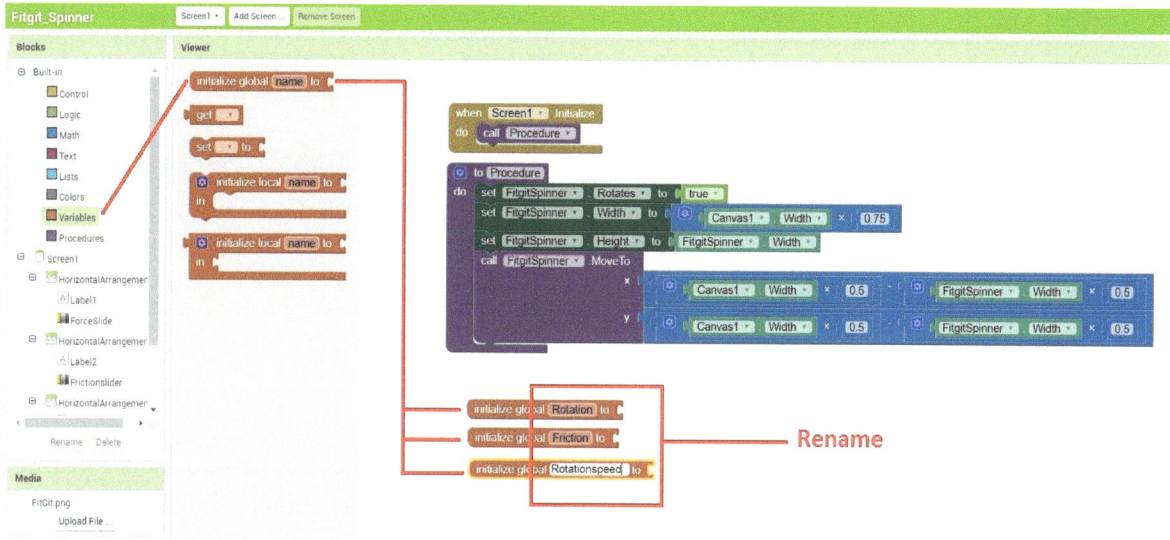

Step 14.1:

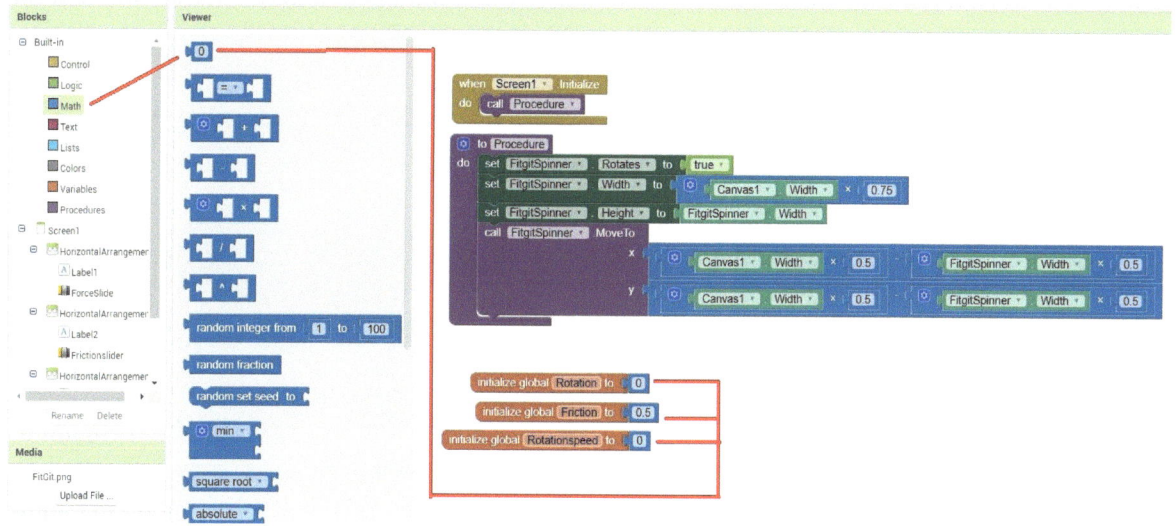

Make Rotation value → 0

Friction Value → 0.5

RotationSpeed → 0

Step 15:

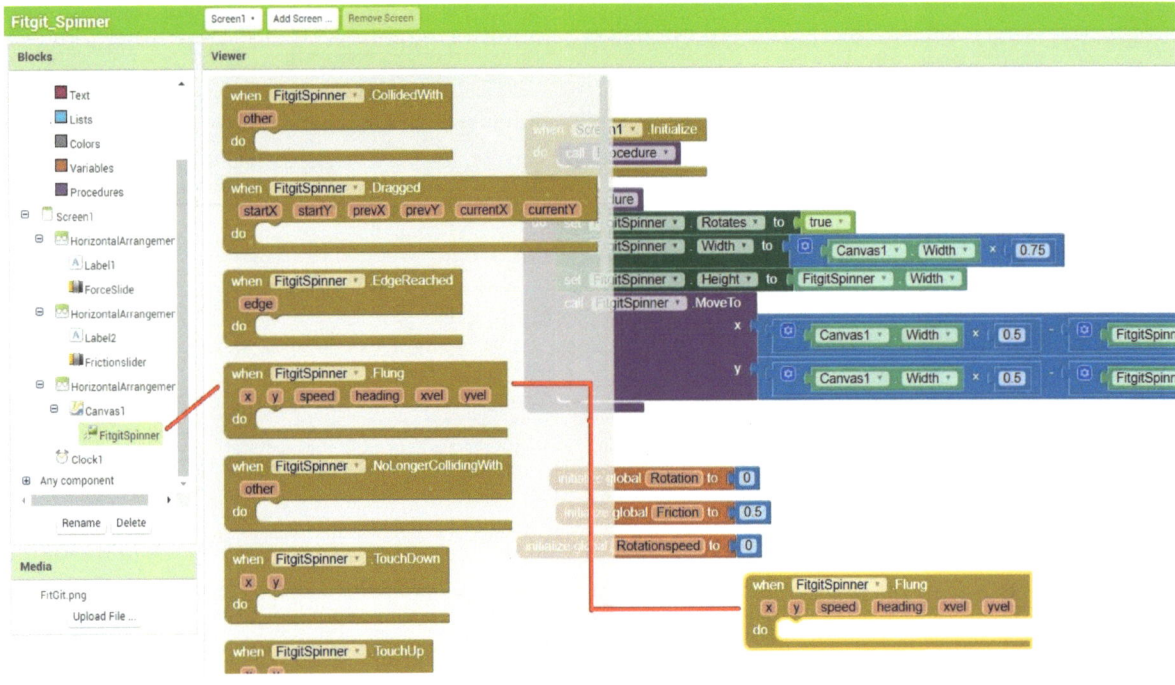

Step 16:

When you place the arrow on the Rotationspeed, You will get Two options get and set -→ place the set method for our required area

Step 17:

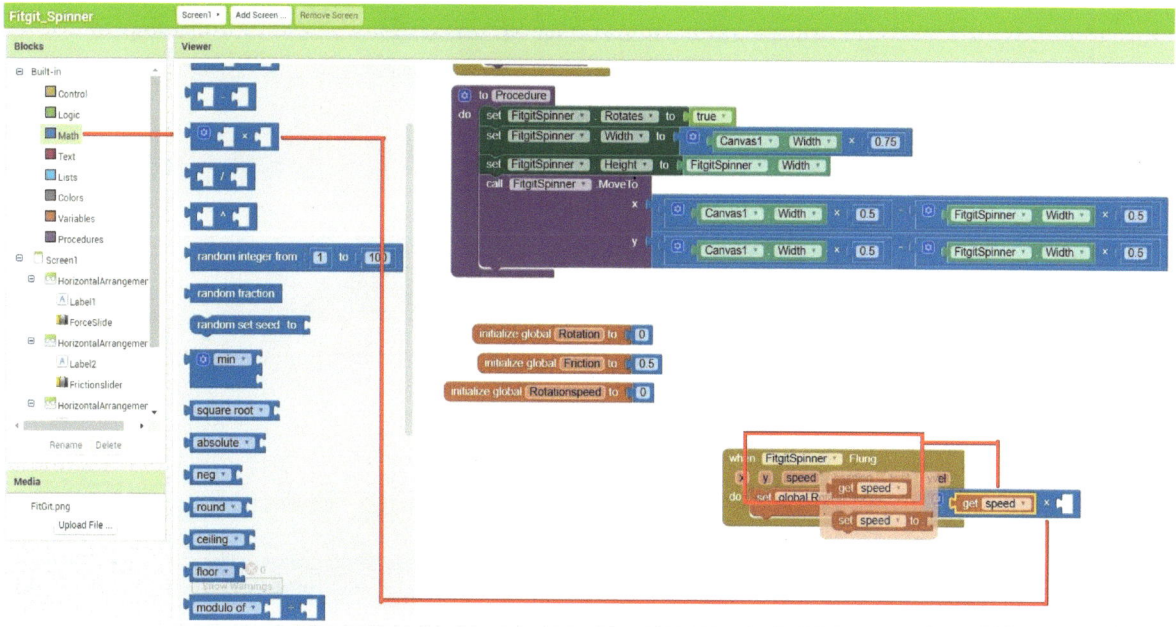

Step 18:

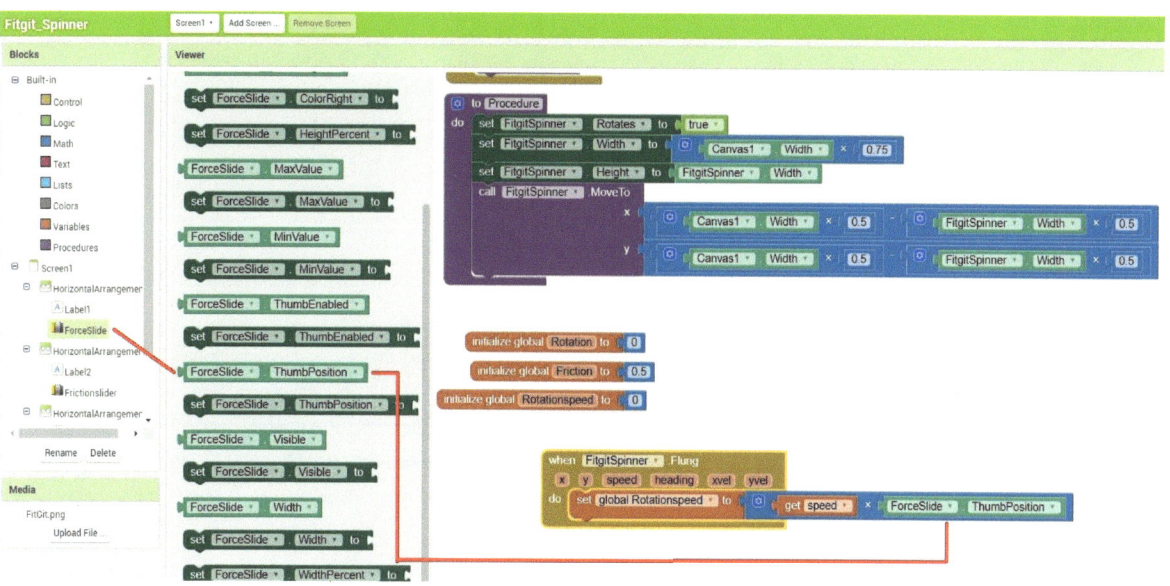

Step 19:

Step 20:

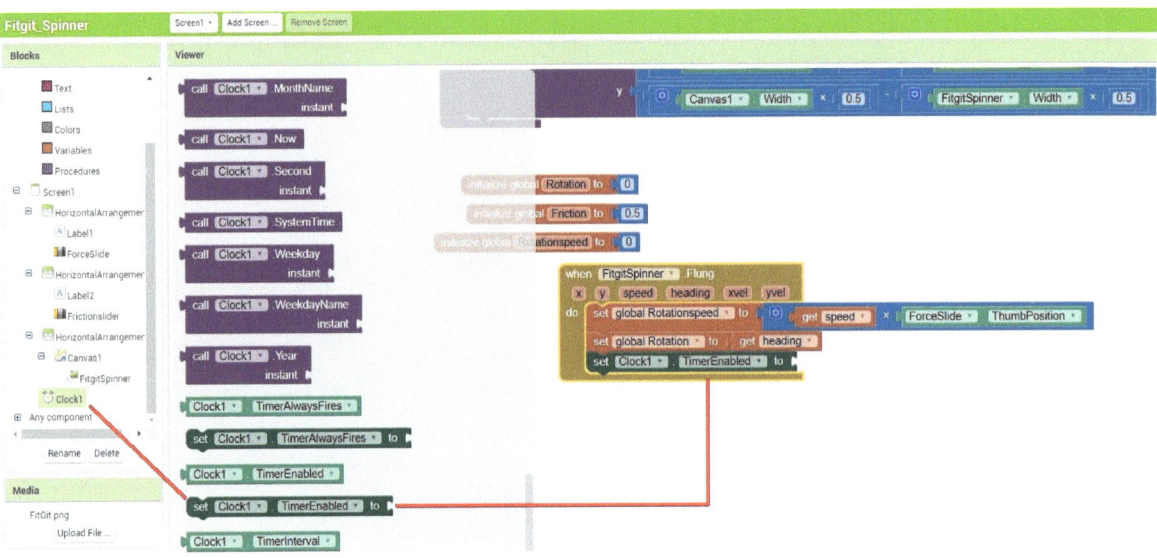

Step 20.1:

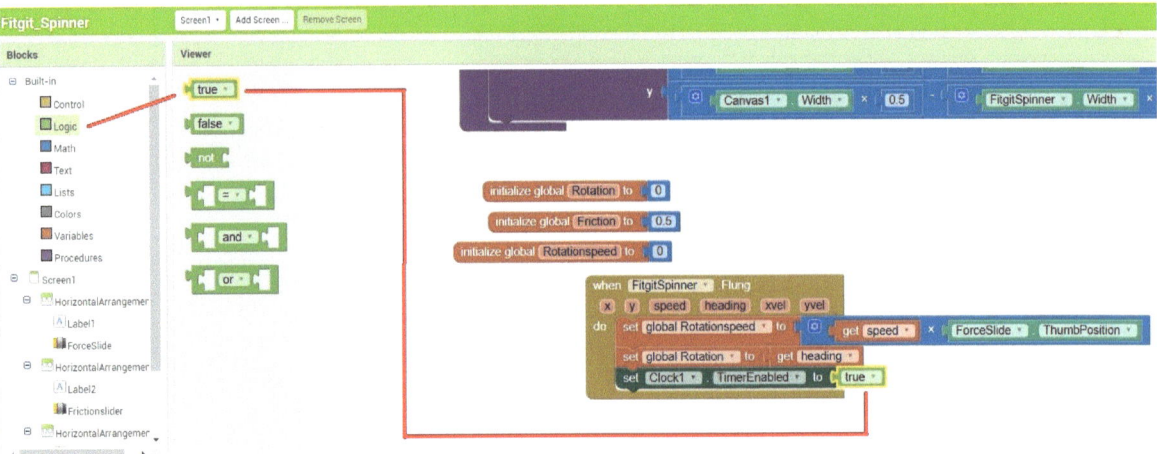

Step 21:

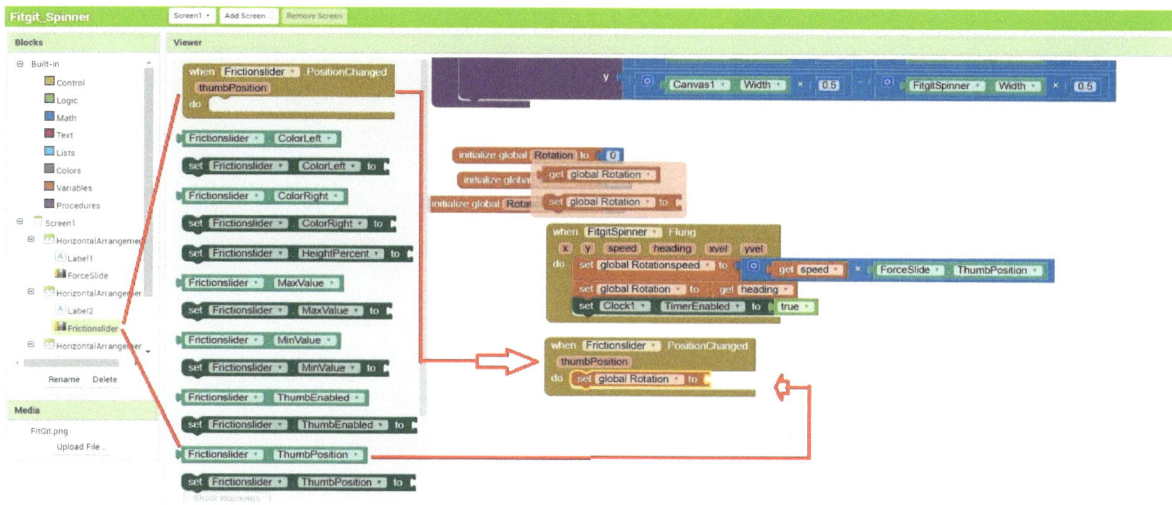

Step 21:

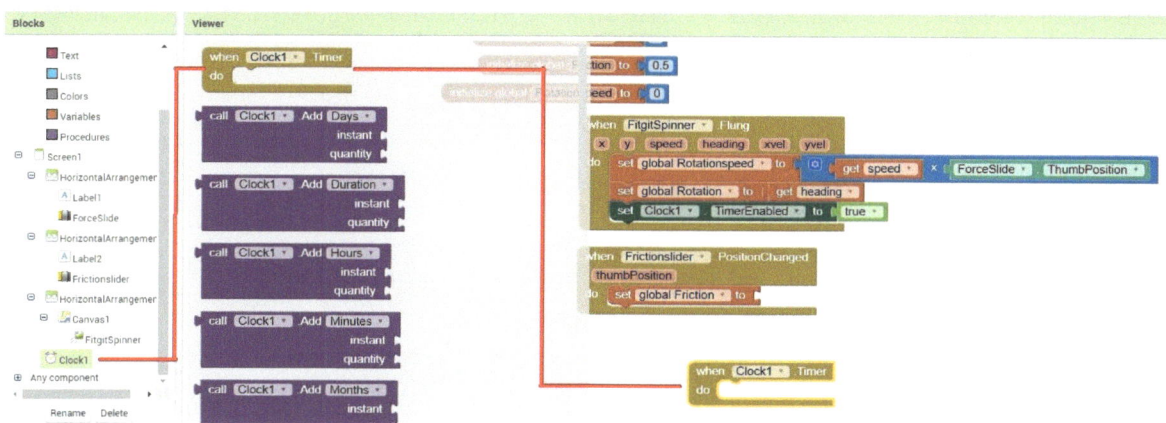

Step 22:

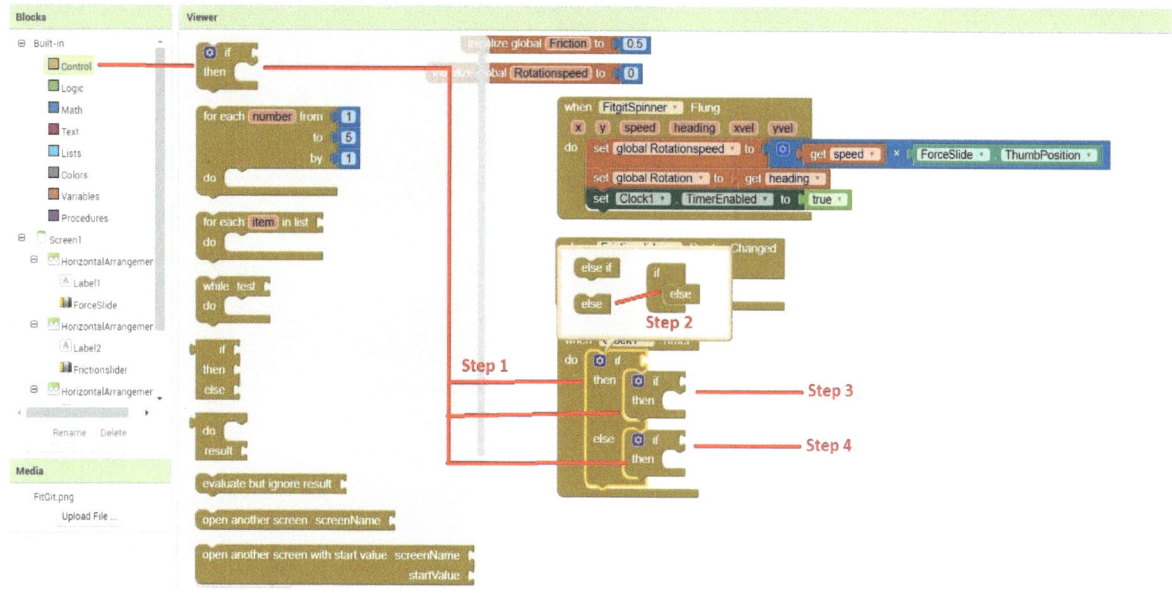

Step 23.1:

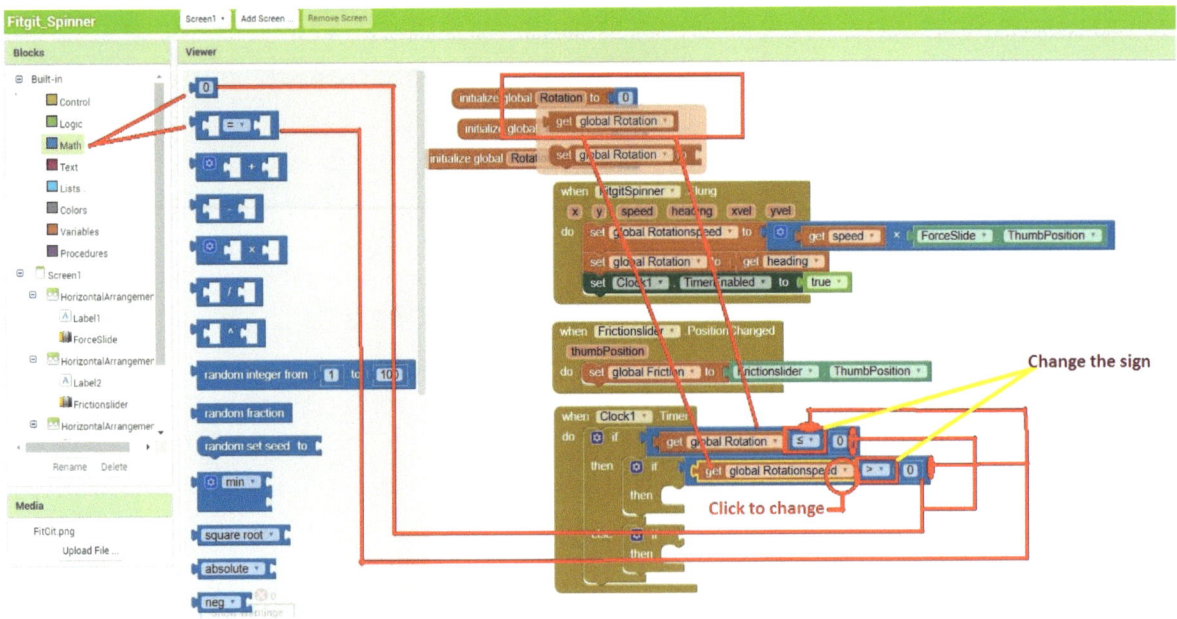

Step 24:

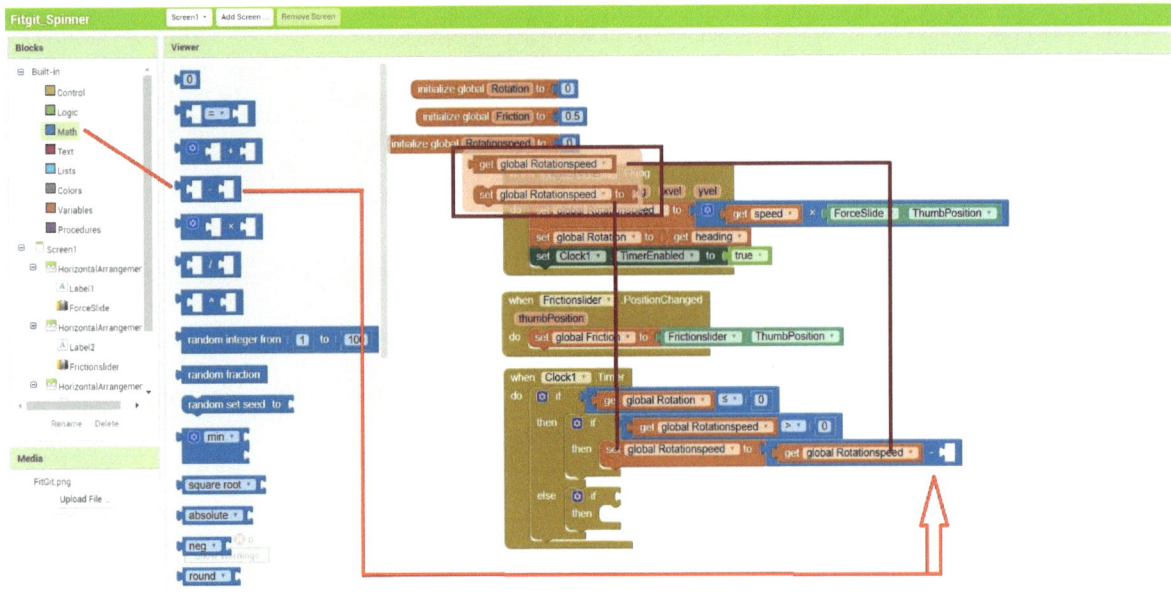

Step 24.1:

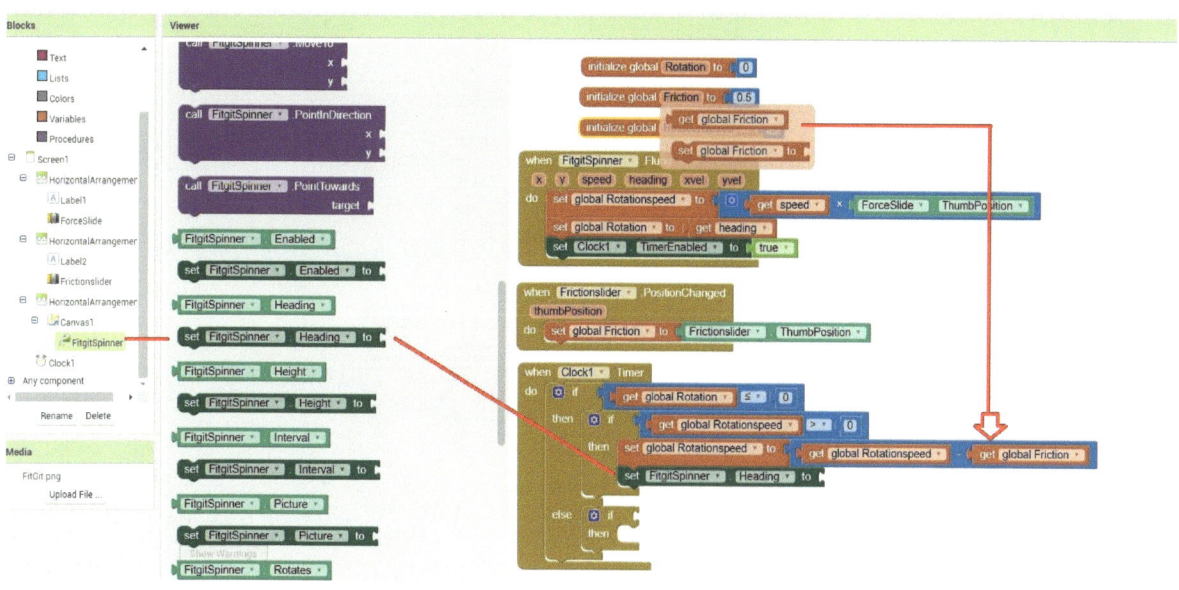

Step 24.2:

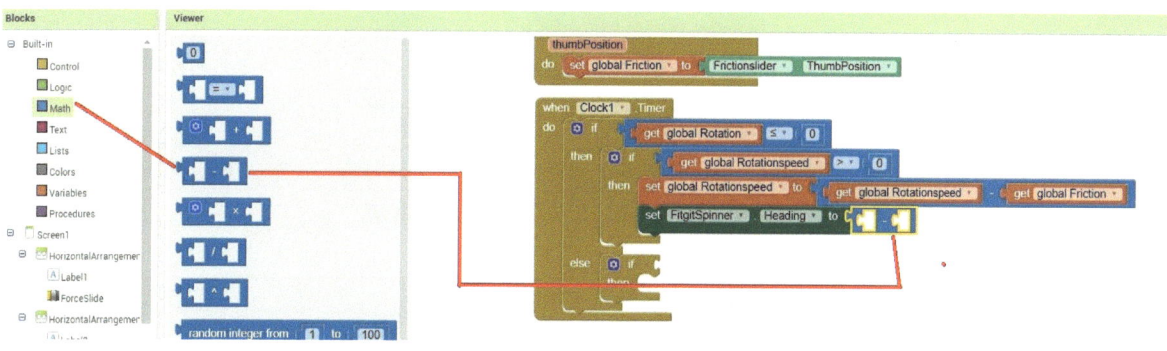

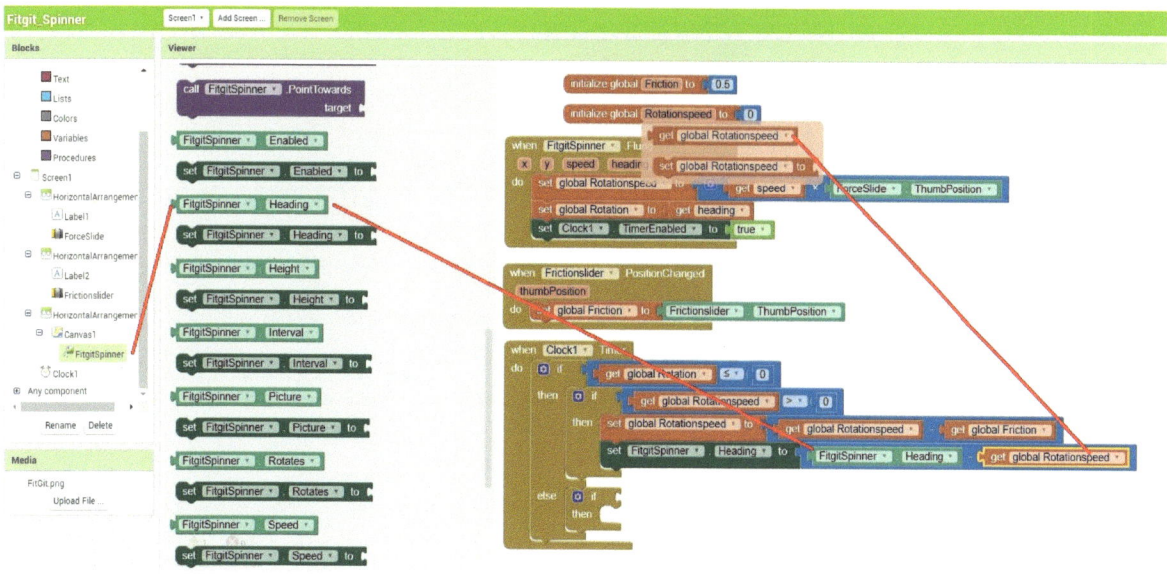

Step 25:

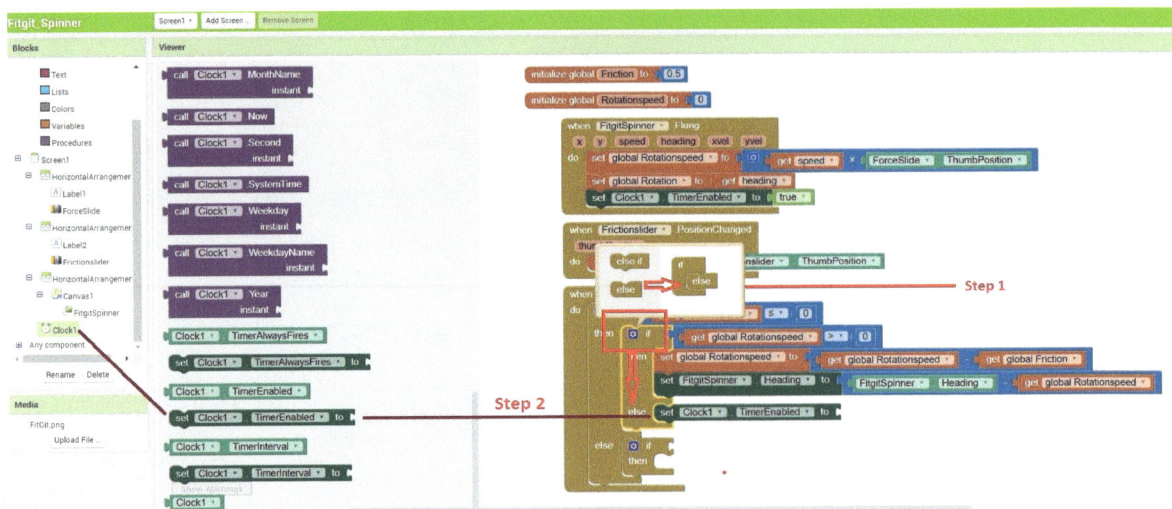

Step 25.1:

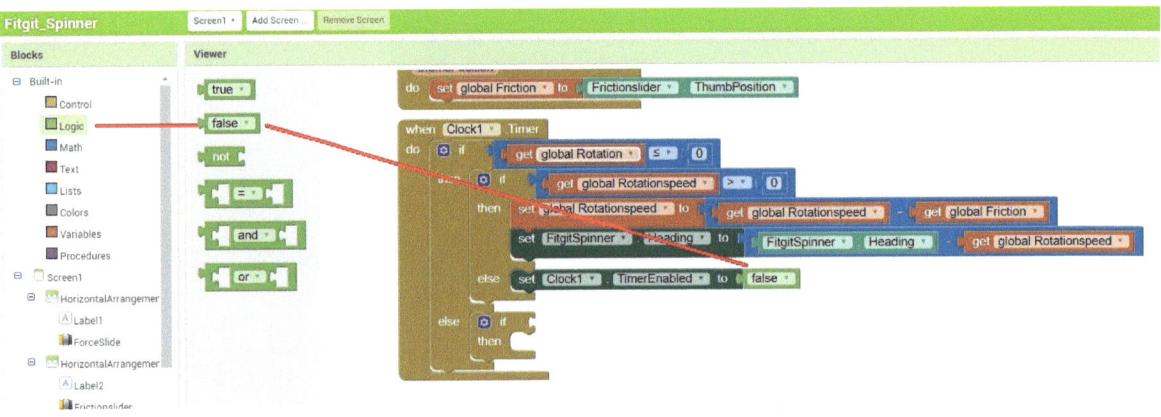

Step 26:

Step 26.1:

Step 27:

Step 1: Separate the blocks

Step 2: Delete this

Step 27.1:

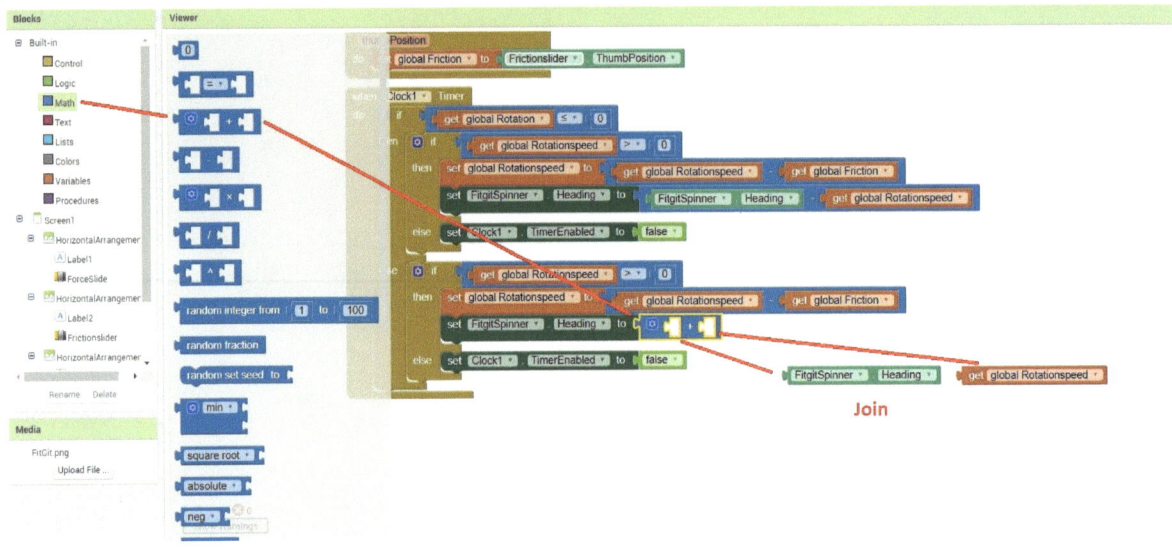

Step 27.2:

Now build as Apk

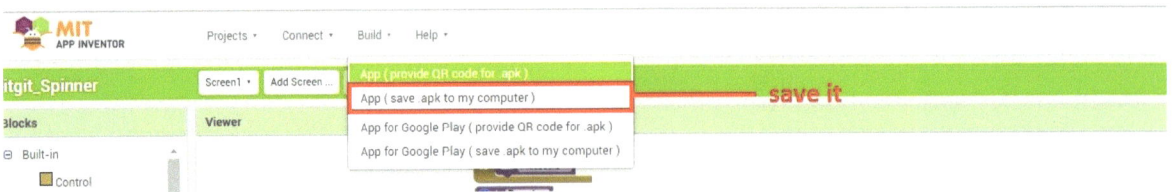

This is the complete blocks verify that

```
when Screen1.Initialize
do  call Procedure

to Procedure
do  set FitgitSpinner.Rotates to true
    set FitgitSpinner.Width to (Canvas1.Width × 0.75)
    set FitgitSpinner.Height to FitgitSpinner.Width
    call FitgitSpinner.MoveTo
        x: (Canvas1.Width × 0.5) - (FitgitSpinner.Width × 0.5)
        y: (Canvas1.Width × 0.5) - (FitgitSpinner.Width × 0.5)

initialize global Rotation to 0
initialize global Friction to 0.5
initialize global Rotationspeed to 0

when FitgitSpinner.Flung
  x y speed heading xvel yvel
do  set global Rotationspeed to (get speed × ForceSlide.ThumbPosition)
    set global Rotation to get heading
    set Clock1.TimerEnabled to true

when Frictionslider.PositionChanged
  thumbPosition
do  set global Friction to Frictionslider.ThumbPosition

when Clock1.Timer
do  if (get global Rotation ≤ 0)
    then
        if (get global Rotationspeed > 0)
        then
            set global Rotationspeed to (get global Rotationspeed - get global Friction)
            set FitgitSpinner.Heading to (FitgitSpinner.Heading - get global Rotationspeed)
        else
            set Clock1.TimerEnabled to false
    else
        if (get global Rotationspeed > 0)
        then
            set global Rotationspeed to (get global Rotationspeed - get global Friction)
            set FitgitSpinner.Heading to (FitgitSpinner.Heading + get global Rotationspeed)
        else
            set Clock1.TimerEnabled to false
```

End Model : Finally, we have created this application front end in mobile and it worked

If you want any other Application development like this, You can Approach us … We will create the application in same way for easy understanding …

www.ingramcontent.com/pod-product-compliance
Lightning Source LLC
Chambersburg PA
CBHW042322250526
R18347200002B/R183472PG45473CBX00007B/5